Light & Easy For Two!

SMART EATING FOR LIFE

Microwave/Conventional Cooking Instructions

by
Lee Harvey, B. Sc., R.P.Dt., RD
&
Helen Chambers, B.Sc., R.P.Dt.

Light & Easy For Two!
By
Lee Harvey & Helen Chambers

Second Printing - June 1991
Third Printing - March 1993
Fourth Printing - March 1994
Fifth Printing - March 1996

Copyright© 1990 by
H. C. Publishing
P. O. Box 3231, Station "D"
Ottawa, Ontario
Canada   K1P 6H8

Canadian Cataloguing in Publication Data

Harvey, Lee, 1935-
  Light & easy for two!

  ISBN 0-9692369-3-X

1. Cookery for two.   2. Low-calorie diet -
Recipes.   I. Chambers Helen, 1934-.   II. Title.

RM222.2.H388 1990   641.5/61   C90-097155-X

Photography by
Gary Carter
Garry Carter Photography Limited
Ottawa, Ontario

Dishes and Accessories courtesy of:
Domus, Ottawa
McIntosh and Watts Ltd., Ottawa

Printed and Produced in Canada by
Friesen Printers
a Division of D.W. Friesen & Sons Ltd.
Altona, Manitoba
Canada
R0G 0B0

Front Cover — Key Lime Pie, page 166

TABLE OF CONTENTS

INTRODUCTION

"Smart eating for life" is becoming easier and more enjoyable. It is not a fad, but a recognized part of a healthy lifestyle. Sound nutrition promotes disease prevention and enables one to enjoy all stages of life more fully.

"Light & Easy For Two!" will guide you in developing your own smart eating style. It includes:

- Recipes especially designed for two
- Tips for a healthy nutritional lifestyle
- How to safely handle and store perishables
- How to keep produce fresh and tasty longer
- Tips for seniors
- Sample menus

ACKNOWLEDGEMENTS

We are indebted to our clients, who continue to test our recipes and offer their comments, and to our families, who provide moral support throughout the process of writing and testing.

Though they are listed inside the front cover of each of our three books, we would like to give special thanks to our food stylist, Margo Embury of Regina, and to our photographer, Garry Carter of Ottawa.

We are grateful to McIntosh and Watts Ltd. and Domus of Ottawa, for lending us china and glassware to enhance our photos. The setting adds a great deal to the presentation of a meal and their help was invaluable.

SMART EATING FOR LIFE

The old familiar story of using **moderation, variety** and **balance** may seem dull compared with the latest food fads, but if something sounds too good to be true, it probably is. Nutrition attracts a lot of quacks, and one must learn to distinguish between the truth and the myths. Instead of looking for the quick fix, concentrate on the smaller easy-to-live-with changes that add up to a long-term improvement in your eating habits.

NUTRIENTS NEEDED

We sit down to a meal of food, not nutrients. But our food should be the conveyor of the 40-50 different nutrients that the body needs in order to perform its many tasks. Since there is no one food that supplies them all, it is important to incorporate a variety of foods into one's diet and in the proper amounts. This is where food guides come in handy. A food guide provides us with groups of foods containing similar nutrients. Our daily menu should contain selections from each food group and as much variety as possible from within food groups. The sample menus on pages 32 to 37 illustrate how this can be done.

Advances in food science, and in the world marketplace, have provided us with a vast variety of foods. Seasonal foods are now available year round, many lean cuts of meats are suitable for a variety of methods of preparation. Foods from around the world may be purchased in supermarkets, and low-fat versions of basic foods are appearing in large numbers.

FAT IN THE DIET

"There are no bad foods, just bad diets." In other words, most healthy individuals can enjoy a wide range of foods. You may need to have some less often than others or eat smaller portions, but the so called "bad" foods do not have to be entirely eliminated from the diet.

One of the most important nutrition guidelines is that the fat content of our diet should not exceed 30% of total calories. This amounts to about 33 grams of fat per 1,000 calories.

The following chart shows, at a glance, the grams of fat in a typical 2,000 calorie day. Only the foods containing fat have been listed.

FOODS CONTAINING FAT		FAT (grams)	PROTEIN (grams)
Lean Roast Beef	4 oz.	12	28
Cheddar Cheese	2 oz.	20	14
Milk 2%	2 cups	10	16
Butter/Margarine	4 tsp.	20	0
Salad Dressing	1 tbsp.	05	0
	Total	67	58

This illustrates how quickly fat adds up and that one must observe moderation in fat consumption. Lowering fat consumption is becoming easier to do because of the many low-fat products appearing on the market. Make good use of these and the other information provided in the Food Group section of this book, pages 21 to 30. Observe the portion sizes for the Fat Group listed on page 29. Those interested in more information on the different types of fats, and additional recipes that emphasize low-fat cooking, please refer to our second book, "Eat Light & Love It!"

A moderate fat intake is recommended for many reasons. A diet high in fat is associated with an increased risk of heart disease and certain types of cancer. A gram of fat contains twice as many calories as a gram of carbohydrate and/or protein. Therefore, fat content also requires careful attention in weight-reduction diets.

PROTEIN

If 30% of total calories are fat calories, derived from a variety of meats, fish, dairy products and visible fat, you are almost ensured of an adequate supply of protein. Please refer to the chart, page 6, to see the grams of protein in some typical fat-containing foods. When you add to this the protein obtained from the plant sources, you more than meet your protein requirements. For instance, the protein requirements for someone weighing 165 pounds is 60 grams or approximately 15% of total calories.

CARBOHYDRATE

The other macronutrient in our diet is carbohydrate. This refers to both complex carbohydrates and to simple sugars which, taken together, should account for about 55% of caloric intake. The menus on pages 32 to 37 will help you relate these percentages to your food intake.

Some common sources of carbohydrates.

Complex Carbohydrate	**Simple Sugar**
Fruit	Fruit
Grains: breads, cereals, pasta	Milk
Vegetables:	Sweeteners:
all types including	sugar, honey
potatoes and legumes	and syrups

It should be noted that sweeteners are referred to as empty calories because they provide few nutrients other than calories.

FIBER

Complex carbohydrates provide us with many essential nutrients, including fiber. Fiber is found in plant foods only, and is the part that humans are not able to digest completely.

Before the oat bran craze, fiber was synonymous with wheat bran. Now there is a greater awareness of the different types of fiber, soluble and insoluble, and the characteristics and sources of each.

Water-soluble fiber appears to help maintain appropriate blood sugar levels, and research has shown that it may help to reduce elevated cholesterol. Many foods contain this type of fibre; oat bran is the best known. But legumes, fruits and many root vegetables, contain a certain amount of water-soluble fibre.

Water-insoluble fiber helps to prevent constipation and, therefore, the medical problems associated with chronic constipation. Besides wheat bran, other good sources are whole-grain breads and cereals, and many fruits and vegetables.

If you increase your intake of fiber, it is important that you do so gradually, and also increase your water intake.

WATER

Water is often referred to as the 'forgotten nutrient.' We form habits of eating meals at certain times of the day and we should do the same in regards to water. Our thirst mechanism is not always sensitive enough to remind us to drink the amount that we really need, which is 6-8 glasses daily. A suggested pattern might be 1 cup (250 mL) upon arising, 1 cup (250 mL)with each meal and 1 cup (250 mL) between meals. It is important to remember that caffeine-containing beverages act as mild diuretics. These draw fluid out of the body, and should not be included in your allowance for the day.

Just as we have a great variety of foods available, there are several sources of water: bottled waters, carbonated and non-carbonated. There are also water filters of various types and plain tap water. If the flavour of tap water does not please, simply add a slice of lemon or lime.

During exercise and warm weather, fluid replacement is even more important.

8

LIFESTYLE

Good health is dependent on many factors, some of which are inherited and some of which are the result of our lifestyle. Making a conscious effort to eat a wide variety of nutritious foods, controlling blood cholesterol levels, dealing with stress in a positive way, exercising regularly, using alcohol in moderation, and maintaining body weight within a normal healthy range, are all important factors that we should make a determined effort to incorporate into our lifestyle.

NORMAL BODY WEIGHT

The use of the Body Mass Index is gaining in popularity for determining body weight. This approach emphasizes health over cosmetics. To determine your BMI refer to the chart on page 19.

Don't allow the often quoted statistics on weight loss persuade you that it is a hopeless task. These statistics tend to be based on results from the severely obese, seen in medical clinics, rather than the average person employing the gradual changes in food habits and lifestyle recommended in this book.

EXERCISE

Exercise is an important part of balancing calories consumed with calories expended. Making exercise a normal part of your day is a habit worth forming. Obviously, it is better to find a form of exercise that you enjoy. Here again, variety is the keyword. If you develop a liking for several forms of exercise you are more likely to stay with them.

The amount of exercise required varies from person to person and then, for each person, with age. An appropriate level of exercise should be an important part of everyone's day.

COOKING FOR TWO

— If this is your first time away from home and you have not perfected your cooking skills, you will find the recipes in this book to be straightforward and easy to prepare.

— If you are a two-career couple, and rely on take-out food or eating out for many of your meals, you will find that with a little help from these recipes, you will be able to eat better at home and actually save time and money.

— If after years of cooking for a family, you now find that cooking is more of a bother than a pleasure, don't lose interest in cooking. Accept the challenge of preparing nutritious meals by cooking this light and easy way.

The recipes in "Light & Easy for Two!" are light in calories, fat, salt and sugar. They are easy to prepare in that the methods of preparation are not difficult, the ingredient lists are short and the ingredients are commonly found in most kitchens. Because the recipes are for two portions, you will not be having the same dinner night after night.

For recipes that follow the same principles, but are for 4 or more portions, try our other books. "Lose Weight & Love It!" comes complete with step-by-step instructions for a healthy weight-loss program and "Eat Light & Love It!" has the bonus of an understandable Cholesterol Control Guide.

NUTRITION LABELLING

Because purchasing decisions are often made in the supermarket, food manufacturers realize that nutrition information is a good marketing tool. All ingredients in a product are listed on the label in descending order according to weight. Take advantage of all of the nutrition information to make educated choices while shopping. For example, in Canada the % of milk fat (M.F.) or butter fat (B.F.) is printed on all dairy products. This includes milk, yogurt and cheese. This enables you to try the products lowest in fat from different producers to determine the one that best suits your needs and tastes.

GROCERIES TO HAVE ON HAND

The use of a printed shopping list, of your own design or one that you purchase, is very helpful in organizing grocery shopping. If possible, have the items appear in the same order on your list as they are found in the supermarket.

The following is a list of useful items to have on hand, whether you are setting up your first kitchen or equipping the kitchen in your retirement home or recreational vehicle.

Staples
beverage: tea, coffee, etc.
cereal: hot and cold
cooking oil
dried fruit: raisins, prunes
flour
mayonnaise
mustard
pasta
peanut butter
rice
salad dressing
skim milk powder
spices, including salt and
 pepper
syrup
sugar, white and brown

Canned Goods
beans: baked and kidney
corn niblets
fish: tuna and salmon
soup
spaghetti sauce
tomatoes

Perishables
breads
butter/margarine
cheese
eggs
fruit, including orange juice
meats: ground meat, chicken
milk
vegetables
yogurt

More Useful Information

Quantity of raw or dry foods to yield 1 cup (250 mL).

Rice, long-grain white:
 ⅓ cup (75 mL) raw, cooked in ⅔ cup (150 mL) water.
Rice, brown:
 ⅓ cup (75 mL) raw, cooked in 1 cup (250 mL) water.
Beans, Lentils and Split Peas:
 ⅓ cup (75 mL) dry, soaked and cooked in water
Macaroni:
 ½ cup (125 mL) dry, cooked in boiling water.
Spaghetti:
 2 oz. (60 g) dry pasta, cooked in boiling water.
Cheese:
 3 oz. (85 g) Parmesan yields 1 cup (250 mL) grated.
 4 oz. (115 g) Cheddar yields 1 cup (250 mL) grated.

FOOD SAFETY

We depend on government regulations to protect us as far as food additives, preservatives and pesticides are concerned. But each year, many cases of food poisoning occur in the home because of improper handling of perishables. Food does not have to look or smell "off" to be unsafe for consumption. With proper storage, handling and cooking of perishables, spoilage and food-borne illnesses can be prevented.

Food Handling

Hands should be washed with soap and hot water before beginning any food preparation.

Raw Meats

A great deal of care must be taken when working with all raw meats. All utensils, such as cutting boards, knives, serving plates and the cook's hands should be washed with soap and hot water to avoid spreading bacteria found in raw meats. This is especially true of raw poultry, which can have high levels of salmonella bacteria. Some authorities do not recommend the use of wooden cutting boards when working with raw poultry, because of the difficulty in thoroughly cleaning them.

All frozen meats should be thawed in the refrigerator rather than at room temperature.

Poultry should be cooked in an oven set no lower than 325°F (160°C) and until the internal temperature reads 180°F (90°C) or until the juices show no sign of pinkness.

All meats should be cooked in one continuous operation.

Eggs

Because of the concern over salmonella, raw eggs should not be consumed and some authorities suggest that eggs should be cooked until both yolk and whites are firm. Cracked or soiled eggs should be discarded.

Storage of Meat, Fish, Eggs and Dairy Products

The following table gives recommended length of time, temperature and packaging for storage.

Food Item	Recommended Storage Time	Handling suggestions
Meat:		
Roasts, steaks and chops	3-4 days	Refrigerate at 34-36°F or 1-2°C
Sausage	2-3 days	Supermarket packaging should be covered with plastic wrap or plastic bag.
Ground meat, stew meat, & variety meats, such as liver & giblets	1-2 days	
Packaged Meats	Check label for best-before date.	
Poultry:		
Whole or cut-up	2-3 days	Remove from store packages, rinse, dry & rewrap loosely with plastic, wax paper or foil.
Ground poultry	1-2 days	
Fish:		
Filets or steaks, raw	2-3 days	Wipe surface with a damp cloth, pat dry and wrap in wax paper or place in a container and seal. Store in the coldest part of refrigerator at 34-36°F or 1-2°C
Mussels, live	7-10 days	
Oysters, live	up to 6 weeks	
Shrimps, scallops	1-2 days	
Eggs:	check carton for best-before date	Store in refrigerator at 36-40°F or 2-4°C

Dairy Foods:

Milk	check carton for best-before date.	Refrigerate at no higher that 40°F or 4°C. Store on refrigerator shelf rather than door. Avoid exposure to light.
Yogurt	check carton for best-before date.	If yogurt separates, simply stir to recombine.

Cheese:

Fresh: Cottage & Cream	Check carton for best-before date.	Refrigerate at 40°F or 4°C If mold has formed on fresh or soft cheese or is throughout a firm one, discard the cheese.
Soft: Brie & Camembert	Approx. 1 week	Remove excess moisture on semi-soft, firm and hard cheese and wrap carefully.
Semisoft: Mozzarella	2-3 weeks	
Firm: Cheddar, Farmer's	5 weeks	
Hard: Parmesan, Romano	up to 10 months	

Storage of Fresh Vegetables

Since vegetables do not ripen after harvesting, most vegetables require **refrigeration,** in the **unwashed** state and then should be **wrapped in plastic.**

Routinely check vegetables that are in storage and discard spoiled items. The following are a few special notes on vegetables that are in addition to or as an exception to the above rule.

Asparagus:	wrap cut ends in a damp paper towel & store as noted above.
Beets:	cut off tops and store as noted above.
Bok Choy:	best used as soon as possible but should be stored as noted above.
Corn:	best used the same day as picked, if not, wrap in damp paper towels and refrigerate in plastic.
Fresh Herbs:	rinse and shake dry, wrap in dry cloth or paper. Refrigerate in plastic. These may be frozen for longer storage.
Garlic:	store unwrapped in a cool, dry, dark place with good ventilation.
Mushrooms:	wrap in paper towels and refrigerate, unwashed, in plastic.
Onions:	store, unwrapped, in a cool, dry, dark place with good ventilation.
Potatoes:	all kinds require cool, dry, dark, well-ventilated storage
Rutabagas:	store, unwrapped, in a cool dry, dark place with good ventilation
Salad Greens:	rinse in cold water and dry well. Wrap in paper towels and refrigerate in plastic.
Spinach/Swiss Chard:	wash in large amounts of cold water and drain. If cooking immediately do not dry, as enough water will remain on the leaves for cooking without adding more water. If storing pat dry and wrap in cloth or paper and refrigerate.
Tomatoes:	store, unwashed, at room temperature until slightly soft, then refrigerate, unwrapped.
Winter Squash:	whole, all kinds require cool, dry, dark, well-ventilated storage.

FOOD STORAGE (Cont'd.)

Storage of Fresh Fruit

Some fruits do not ripen after picking and should be purchased ripe. They should be refrigerated, unwashed, in paper or plastic bags. Other fruits will ripen if left at room temperature. Some should be left uncovered, others ripen more quickly if loosely packed in a paper bag. For more information about specific fruits, see numbered notes.

Kind of Fruit	Ripens After Picking
Apples (1)	yes
Apricots	yes, covered
Avocados (2)	yes, until cut
Bananas (3)	yes, uncovered
Berries (4)	no
Cherries (4)	no
Citrus Fruit	no, may have limited room temp. storage
Kiwi	yes, uncovered
Grapes	no
Guavas	yes, uncovered
Litchees	no
Mangoes	yes, uncovered
Melons (5)	yes, until cut
Nectarines	yes, uncovered
Papayas	yes, covered
Peaches	yes, covered
Pears	yes, covered, may need 3-7 days
Pineapple (6)	yes, uncovered
Plums	yes, covered
Pomegranates (7)	no

(1) While most fruits may be stored in paper or plastic, apples should be refrigerated in plastic bags in order to retain crispness.

(2) Avocados once ripened or cut should be stored in a paper or plastic bag and refigerated. The cut surface should be rubbed with lemon juice to prevent browning.

(3) Ripe bananas may be stored in the refrigerator to preserve the flesh. Only the skin will turn brown.

(4) Because berries and cherries are fragile fruits, they need to be stored with care. Refrigerate unwashed fruit in a shallow pan lined with paper towels. Cover the fruit with additional paper towels and then plastic wrap.

(5) Melons give off a gas once they are ripe or are cut and for that reason should be stored in a tightly sealed plastic bag.

(6) Pineapple may become softer and juicier after picking but not sweeter. To ensure a good pineapple, look for the following: jet-shipped label, large, plump fruit, fresh looking with the color of the rind varying from green to golden.

(7) Pomegranates may be stored for short periods of time at room temperature or refrigerated in plastic for longer. The seeds may be frozen.

Fresh Produce

Produce shopping for two may require extra care, since it may not be eaten quickly. With proper storage, most produce can be stored for at least a week and many for longer periods.

BMI

BMI (Body Mass Index) is a means of measuring body fatness. Developed by Quetelet in the 19th Century (and sometimes referred to as the Quetelet Index), it is indices of weights associated with wellness or absence of disease, in adults, 20-65 years of age. Many methods of measuring body fatness have been developed in the last few years, from skinfold measurements to water immersion, but none have been more accurate and as practical and easy to use for the population at large, as the BMI. Heights and weights are easy measurements to obtain and they are all that are necessary to calculate BMI.

The formula is $\dfrac{\textbf{weight (in kilograms)}}{\textbf{(height in meters)}^2}$ **or** $\dfrac{\textbf{wt. kg}}{\textbf{ht. M}^2}$

One might ask, if this is such an old measurement, why are we only beginning to use it now? One reason is our preoccupation with thinness, especially predominant in North American women. Consequently, many women strive for unrealistic body weights and find them impossible to achieve.

unrealistic weight goals---

frustrated people trying to achieve
unrealistic goals---

fad diets---

poor eating habits---

It becomes a vicious circle.

Conversely, many men are surprised when they calculate their BMI and learn that their weight is **higher** than recommended! This determination can help them to realize that their excess pounds could be detrimental to their health.

Most people fall within a healthy weight range, yet more than 50% of the population are concerned about their weight. Calculating your BMI can help you put your present weight into perspective. If your weight falls within the healthy range, you can turn your concerns to eating healthfully and getting enough exercise to keep it that way.

Use the following chart and calculate your BMI.

If your weight falls within the healthy zone, congratulations! "Light & Easy for Two!" can help you maintain a healthy weight and normal cholesterol level.

If your BMI is **below** 20, and has been for a number of years, it may be that you are one of the tiny people with small bones. Don't worry about it. You're probably O.K. If your BMI has fallen below 20 in a short period of time, consult your physician to determine if there is a medical reason for the drop.

If your BMI is **above** 25, you can set a realistic goal weight and work towards it. Our first book, "Lose Weight & Love It!," can help you set up a sensible, safe weight-loss program. "Eat Light & Love It!" and this book can provide you with more recipes. When you attain your goal, all of these recipes will help you to maintain your new smart-eating style.

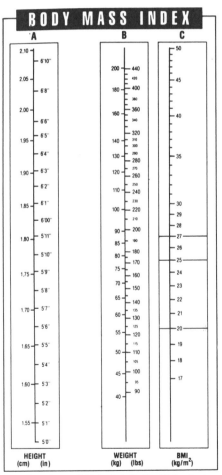

Source: Expert Group on Weight Standards, Health and Welfare Canada

HOW TO FIND YOUR BMI — IT'S EASY

1. Mark an X at your height on line A.
2. Mark an X at your weight on line B.
3. Take a ruler and join the two X's.
4. To find your BMI, draw a line to C.

FOR EXAMPLE:
- If Michael is 5'11" (1.80 m) and weighs 188 lbs. (85 kg), his BMI is about 26.
- If Irene is 5'4" (1.60 m), weighs 132 lbs. (60 kg), her BMI is about 23.

Under 20 A BMI under 20 may be associated with health problems for some individuals. It may be a good idea to consult a dietitian and physician for advice.

20-25 This zone is associated with the lowest risk of illness. This is the preferred range.

25-27 A BMI over 25 may be associated with health problems for some people. Caution is suggested if your BMI is in this zone.

Over 27 A BMI over 27 is associated with increased risk of health problems such as heart disease, high blood pressure and diabetes. It may be a good idea to consult a dietitian and physician.

THE CANADIAN
DIETETIC
ASSOCIATION
AND THE
DIETITIANS OF
YOUR PROVINCE
EAT WELL, LIVE WELL

From material produced by
The Canadian Dietetic Association, 1988

TIPS FOR SENIORS

For several reasons, our caloric requirements may diminish as we grow older. This may be due to a decrease in physical activity or it may be because the aging process brings about a change in the ratio of lean body mass to fat tissue. Fat tissue requires fewer calories, than lean tissue, to maintain itself.

MEDICAL PROBLEMS

Many medical problems require some changes in food habits. These should be explained as part of the treatment, and may require careful planning to maintain a balanced diet. Other conditions, such as arthritis, have attracted many diet theories that have not been proven scientifically. It is important for those with arthritis to keep their weight normal, so that weight-bearing joints have no added strain.

CONSTIPATION

Constipation may be a problem at any age, but perhaps more so as body processes begin to slow down. A high-fiber diet and exercise should be used instead of laxatives, whenever possible, to remedy this. There are many high fiber foods. Cereals, because of the variety now available, can be used in a way that would suit most individual tastes. This might be hot cereal made from multigrains, with wheat bran added, (increase gradually) or cold cereal with a high fiber content (10-12 grams of fibre per serving). Whole fruits and vegetables, with skins on, and lots of water should be included.

INTEREST IN FOOD

If your interest in food has decreased, along with the number of people sitting at your dinner table, now is the time for you to reestablish a positive attitude towards food. You may regularly share meals with others or prepare a little extra for someone who lives alone or for your married children, if they are working. New table accessories, a simple floral arrangement, a change of table linens, throwing away your chipped dishes and enjoying your good ones, or even eating in a different location such as outside on a patio or balcony, may increase your enjoyment of food and food preparation.

INTRODUCTION TO THE RECIPES & FOOD GROUPS

The recipes that follow should help you attain, or maintain, a healthy eating style.

These recipes are also designed to fit into a **weight-loss program,** a **cholesterol-control program,** and a **diabetic diet.** The Food Group designation for each recipe is for this purpose. These groups are explained in the Food Group section of this book. It is designed to guide you toward eating healthful quantities of foods at each meal, and to show you which food groups are contained in that particular recipe.

For example, The Barley Burger Stew on page 75 provides you with foods from the meat, bread and vegetable groups. To make a complete meal you could add fruit, a dairy food and probably another selection from the bread group. If you are following a diabetic diet, you will find these food groups are very similar to those of the diabetic association. except we have separated the fruits and vegetables into two groups. If you are presently following the weight-loss program described in our first book, "Lose Weight & Love It!", or the cholesterol-control program in our second book, "Eat Light & Love It!", simply add these recipes to your collection. You will have over 100 new, low-fat recipes to help you attain your goals.

You will notice that two or three of our recipes have a higher fat content. It is O.K. to include a higher fat meal in your diet **on occasion.** You can achieve a balance by using a low-fat meal in the same day. This is illustrated in the sample menus for Days 2 and 11. Both illustrate lunches eaten out that are a bit higher in fat, but are balanced by a low-fat fish meal later in the day.

There are one or two recipes we would not recommend for inclusion on a diabetic meal plan, because of the high sugar content. These are indicated at the bottom of the recipes.

Sodium content may be high in a few recipes. This is because of the use of commercial soup bases, olives or canned vegetables. One way of reducing the sodium content is to use low-sodium, low-fat soup base or a homemade stock.

21

When a choice of ingredients is indicated, margarine or butter for instance, the **first** ingredient is the one included in the analysis.

Where ingredients are listed as "optional", they are **not** included in the analysis.

You will notice that we use wine in many of our recipes. Recent research indicates that all of the alcohol does not burn off with cooking. Therefore, we calculate 50% of the wine calories in the nutrient analysis. If you only use wine for cooking and want to keep it fresh, we suggest freezing it in an ice cube tray or pour a bit of olive oil into the bottle slowly. It will form a seal on top of the wine, preventing oxidation and spoilage. To reuse, pour very slowly and the oil will "slip back" as you pour.

We hope that, as you use our recipes, you will begin to see how you can modify your own favorite recipes to fit the low-fat, healthy way of cooking.

Microwave times for cooking vary with temperature of food, the utensil used and the wattage of the oven.

MILK GROUP   TABLE 1

Milk products provide carbohydrates for energy and are our major source of calcium. The fat content can vary widely.

Many people assume that 2% milk is just about the same as skim. But it is not. Homogenized milk is in the range of 3.5% BF. If you don't like skim, 1% is available in many areas. Yogurt is thought of as a healthy food, but before you jump to that conclusion, read the label to see how much milk fat it contains. It can range from less that 1% up to 10%. Again, the lower the better. Find a low-fat yogurt that meets your requirements in flavor and texture. Cultured buttermilk is made from a low-fat milk of less than 1% MF.

One portion is equivalent to the amount listed below.

skim milk .... ½ cup (125 mL)
powdered instant skim milk .... ¼ cup (60 mL)
evaporated skim milk .... ¼ cup (60 mL)
buttermilk.. ½ cup (125 mL)
yogurt, plain, low-fat .... ½ cup (125 mL)

VEGETABLE GROUP   TABLE 2

This group of foods provide minerals, vitamins and fiber, and are relatively low in calories. Use them generously.

Subgroup A: The vegetables listed in this subgroup contain more starch than those in Subgroup B. If you are following a weight loss program, you may use more vegetables from Subgroup B, and have only 1 or 2 servings daily from this group.

beets   ½ cup (125 mL)
Brussels sprouts..................................... ½ cup (125 mL)
carrots .... ½ cup (125 mL)
carrots and peas.................................... ½ cup (125 mL)
mixed vegetables................................... ½ cup (125 mL)
onions, cooked...................................... ½ cup (125 mL)
parsnips... ½ cup (125 mL)
peas, green, canned .... ⅓ cup (75 mL)
peas, fresh or frozen .... ½ cup (125 mL)
pumpkin .... ½ cup (125 mL)
sauerkraut .... 1 cup (250 mL)
snow peas... 10 pods
squash, yellow or winter .... ½ cup (125 mL)
turnips... ½ cup (125 mL)
water chestnuts .... 8 medium

VEGETABLE GROUP   TABLE 2 (Cont'd.)

Subgroup B: Select at least 1 cup (250 mL) cooked per day and eat them raw whenever you like.

artichoke
asparagus
bamboo shoots
beans, green and waxed
bean sprouts
bok choy
broccoli
cabbage
cauliflower
celery
cucumber
eggplant
endive
fiddleheads
kale
kohlrabi

lettuce
mushrooms
okra
onions, green
pepper, green, red
pimiento
radish
spinach and other greens
Swiss chard
tomato, 1 small
canned tomatoes
tomato or vegetable juice
vegetable marrow
watercress
zucchini

FRUIT GROUP   TABLE 3

All fruit portions are listed as fresh, canned or frozen without sugar. These carbohydrate foods provide us with energy, vitamins, minerals and fiber.

apple	½ medium or 1 small
apple juice	⅓ cup (75 mL)
applesauce	½ cup (125 mL)
apricots	2 medium
banana	½ small
berries	½ cup (125 mL)
(blackberries, blueberries, raspberries, Saskatoon berries)	
cantaloupe	¼ small
cherries	10 large
crabapple	1 small
cranberries	1 cup (250 mL)
currants	2 tbsp. (30 mL)
dates	2
fig	1 medium
fresh fruit cup	½ cup (125 mL)
fruit cocktail	½ cup (125 mL)

gooseberries	1 cup (250 mL)
grapefruit	½ small
grapefruit juice	½ cup (125 mL)
grapefruit sections	½ cup (125 mL)
grapes	14
grape juice	¼ cup (60 mL)
honeydew melon	1/10 medium
kiwi fruit	2
mandarine orange	1
mandarine orange sections	½ cup (125 mL)
mango	⅓ medium
nectarine	½ medium
orange	1 small
orange juice	½ cup (125 mL)
orange sections	½ cup (125 mL)
papaya	¼ medium
peach	1 large
pear	1 small
pineapple, fresh, cubed	½ cup (125 mL)
pineapple, canned, crushed or cubes	½ cup (125 mL)
pineapple juice	⅓ cup (75 mL)
pineapple rings, canned	2
plums or prunes	2 medium
pomegranate	½ medium
prune juice	¼ cup (60 mL)
raisins	2 tbsp. (30 mL)
rhubarb, cooked	1 cup (250 mL)
strawberries	1 cup (250 mL)
tangarine	1
watermelon, diced	1 cup (250 mL)

These complex carbohydrate foods are our primary energy source. You can see in the sample menus how many portions we use per day, to meet energy requirements. The amount listed for each food constitutes one serving. You may need to double or triple servings, depending upon the meal, your appetite and how many calories a day it takes to keep your weight at its best level.

This group includes all types of breads, crackers, cereals, starchy vegetables, grains and pastas.

bagel	½
bread	1 slice (25 g)
bread crumbs	¼ cup (60 mL)
bread sticks, plain	4
dinner roll, plain	1
English muffin, crumpet	½
flat breads (RyKrisp etc.)	3
graham wafers (2" or 5 cm sq.)	4
hamburger bun	½
hotdog bun	½
kaiser roll	½
melba toast, round	8
melba toast, rectangular	4
matzos	1
pita bread (8" or 20 cm)	¼
rusk	2
soda crackers	6
tortilla (6" or 15 cm.)	1
cornstarch	2 tbsp. (30 mL)
flour	2½ tbsp. (37 mL)
tapioca	2 tbsp. (30 mL)

cereals:

cooked	½ cup (125 mL)
dry — before cooking	2 tbsp. (30 mL)
cold flakes, unsweetened	¾ cup (175 mL)
cold puffed, unsweetened	1 cup (250 mL)
all-bran or bran buds	½ cup (125 mL)
muffet	1
shredded wheat	1

starchy vegetables:

corn, canned	½ cup (125 mL)
corn, cob	½ large
dry beans, peas, lentils cooked	½ cup (125 mL)
lima beans	½ cup (125 mL)
potatoes	1 small
potatoes, mashed	½ cup (125 mL)
sweet potato	1 small
barley, cooked	½ cup (125 mL)
barley, dry	2 tbsp. (30 mL)
bulgar, kasha, cooked	½ cup (125 mL)
couscous	½ cup (125 mL)
macaroni, cooked	½ cup (125 mL)
rice, spaghetti, noodles	½ cup (125 mL)

snack foods:

popcorn	3 cups (750 mL)
pretzel sticks	20

The following items contain 1 bread serving plus 1 fat serving.*

arrowroot	3
baking powder biscuit (2" or 5 cm)	1
cookies, plain:	
digestive, oatmeal	2
gingersnaps	3
social tea	3
doughnut, cake-type, plain	1
French-fried potatoes	10
soups, canned, diluted with water	1 cup (250 mL)

*These foods should be restricted if the intent is to lower serum cholesterol levels.

Use lean cuts of meat, in particular tenderloin, eye of the round, flank steak, bottom and top round, rump and meats that are low in visible fat. For a really low-fat ground beef, grind it yourself or ask your butcher to grind lean meat only. Or, use ground turkey in recipes that call for ground beef. Boneless turkey breast fillets are now available and make a low-fat, quick-to-prepare and versatile meat. Trim meat before cooking. Broil or roast meats or in the case of ground beef, drain off excess fat.

LEAN MEAT (L MEAT) These meats and alternates contain 1-3 g of fat per portion, less than 10% fat. In many instances one portion is 1 oz. (30 g), for exceptions, see down the list.

lean beef, lamb, veal, pork, ham, poultry without skin	1 oz. (30 g)
*organ meats	1 oz. (30 g)
lean back bacon, pastrami., smoked meat..	1 oz. (30 g)
clams, mussels, oysters, scallops	3 (30 g)
shrimp	5 (30 g)
crab, lobster	¼ cup (30 g)
fish fillets	1 oz. (30 g)
canned tuna, salmon, drained	¼ cup (60 mL) 1 oz. (30 g)
herring	1 oz. (30 g)
sardines	3 (30 g)
smelt	2 medium
cheese 7% M.F.	1 oz. (30 g)
cheese, skim milk slices	1 oz. (30 g)
cheese, cottage, 2% MF or less	¼ cup (60 mL) 2 oz. (55 g)
ricotta cheese 5% M.F.	¼ cup (60 mL) 2 oz. (55 g)
tofu (soy bean curd)	2¼ oz. (75 g)

REGULAR MEATS (R MEAT) These meats and alternates contain 4-7 g of fat (most of which is saturated fat) per portion (less than 20% fat).

luncheon meats, fat-reduced	1 oz. (30 g)
frankfurters, wieners.., fat-reduced	1 oz. (30 g)
mozzarella cheese 15% M.F. (part skim)	1 oz. (30 g)
*cottage cheese	¼ cup (60 mL) 2 oz. (55 g)
processed cheese slices	1 oz. (30 g)
*eggs, medium	1

FATTY MEATS (F MEAT) *These meats and alternates contain extra fat and should be used sparingly.

beef shortribs & spareribs	2 oz. (60 g)
regular corned beef, smoked meat, luncheon meat	1 oz. (30 g)
sausages & frankfurters	1 oz. (30 g)
Cheddar and all other cheeses	1 oz. (30 g)
ricotta cheese 22% M.F	¼ cup (60 mL)
grated Parmesan cheese	3 tbsp. (45 mL)
duck and goose, domestic	1 oz. (30 g)

*Restrict these foods to lower serum cholesterol.

FAT GROUP   LIST 6

These foods are very dense in calories, measure carefully, if you are on a weight-loss plan. Use sparingly otherwise.

Low Saturated Fat

avocado	⅛
cream cheese, light	1½ tbsp. (22 mL)
cooking oil	1 tsp. (5 mL)
margarine, soft P:S ratio 2:1 or better*	1 tsp. (5 mL)
mayonnaise	1 tsp. (5 mL)
mayonnaise, reduced calorie	1 tbsp. (15 mL)
nuts	5 small
olives, large	3
olives, small	5
peanuts	10
peanut butter	½ tbsp. (7 mL)
salad dressings, oil & vinegar style	2 tsp. (10 mL)

High Saturated Fat**

bacon, crisp	1 slice
butter	1 tsp. (5 mL)
light butter	2 tsp. (10 mL)
cream, 10% M.F.	2 tbsp. (30 mL)
cream, 18-22%	1½ tbsp. (22 mL)
cream, whipping	1 tbsp. (15 mL)
cream, sour	2 tbsp. (30 mL)
cream cheese	1 tbsp. (15 mL)
pâté	1 tbsp. (15 mL)
salad dressings, creamy	2 tsp. (10 mL)
salad dressings, cheese	2 tsp. (10 mL)

*   P:S — Polyunsaturated Fat: Saturated Fat
** Restrict these food to lower serum cholesterol levels.   **29**

CALORIE-POOR FOODS   LIST 7

These foods contain little food value and few calories. If you are following a weight-loss program, choose no more than two servings per day.

anchovies 2
barbecue sauce .... 1 tbsp. (15 mL)
bran, natural .... 2 tbsp. (30 mL)
chili sauce .... 1 tbsp. (15 mL)
dietetic fruit spreads .... 1 tsp. (5 mL)
ketchup .... 1 tsp. (5 mL)
*non-dairy coffee whitener .... 1 tsp. (5 mL)
relish .... 1 tsp. (5 mL)
*whipped topping .... 1 tbsp. (15 mL)

*these foods should be restricted if the intent is to lower serum cholesterol levels.

FREE FOODS

These foods may enhance flavor, but contain few calories or little food value. They are called free and may be used as desired.

artificial sweetener
*bouillon
clear broth
coffee
*consommé
dry cocoa
flavoring extracts
gelatin, plain
herbs and spices
horseradish
lemon or lime juice, wedge
mineral water
mustard

parsley
pimientos
soda water
*sour pickles
*soy sauce
sugar-free soft drinks
tea
Tabasco sauce
vinegar
water
Worcestershire sauce

*relatively high in sodium

INTRODUCTION TO THE SAMPLE MENUS

We have provided three (3) sets of sample menus, each at a different calorie level. There is a 2-week menu at each level and the menus coordinate with each other. That is, if you are eating at the 1,500 calorie level and your spouse at the 2,000 calorie level, you change some **amounts** of foods but you can prepare the same basic meal for both of you.

Try the 1,200 calorie menu **IF**
> you are a sedentary female who wants to lose weight.

Try the 1,500 calorie menu **IF**
> you are an active female who wants to lose weight
> you are a sedentary male who wants to lose weight
> you are an older female who wants to maintain her present weight

The 2,000 calorie menu is probably for you **IF**
> you are a young, active female who wants to maintain her present weight
> you are a young active male who wants to lose weight
> you are a moderately active male who wants to maintain his present weight.

All of the menus have been computer analysed and meet recommended proportions of carbohydrate, protein and fat. The carbohydrate, total fat and saturated fat content are noted as percentages of total calories at the bottom of each day. See page 38 for abbreviation code for menus.

I would like you to take a minute and compare the fat content of the 2,000 calorie menu with the 1,200 or the 1,500 calorie levels. Notice how the fat content is at 30% almost every day on the 2,000 calorie menu. That is primarily due to the use of 2% milk instead of skim, regular mayonnaise instead of reduced-calorie mayonnaise, and regular salad dressings instead of diet dressings. There is also more margarine used because of the increased quantities of breads and starches. You can see that by using diet salad dressings and skim milk, we can cut the fat content of our diets quite easily. Think about it.

We hope that you will find these menus helpful in your quest for a healthy lifestyle, through light and easy cooking.

SAMPLE MENU — 1200 CALORIE MENU — WEEK #1

	Day 1	Day 2	Day 3	Day 4	Day 5	Day 6	Day 7
Breakfast	½ banana 1 s. wh. gr. toast ½ T. diet jam 1 c. skim milk	½ c. orange jce. ¾ c. cold cereal 1 c. skim milk	½ c. apple jce. ½ wh. bagel 1 T. lt. cream cheese ½ T. diet jam	½ banana ¾ c. cold cereal 1 c. skim milk	½ c. orange jce. 1 sl. wh. gr. toast 1 poached egg 1 c. skim milk	½ c. grapefruit jce. 2 pancakes 1 tsp. margarine ½ c. applesauce, no sugar 1 c. skim milk	*Quick Breakfast Before Exercise* ½ c. orange jce. 1 sl. wh. gr. toast 1 tsp. margarine ½ T. diet jam
Lunch	sandwich: 2 sl. wh. gr. bread 2 T. peanut butter 1 T. diet jam raw vegetables	*Lunch at Restaurant:* 1 sl. cheese, vegetable pizza salad, lemon juice	sandwich: 2 sl. wh. gr. bread 2 oz. (60 g) drained tuna 1 T. lo-cal. mayo lettuce raw vegetables	1 oz. (30 g) lean ham 1 oz. (30 g) lo-fat cheese on a kaiser roll lettuce, tomato, mustard 1 T. lo-cal. mayo	sandwich: 2 sl. wh. gr. bread 2 oz. (60 g) draied tuna 1 T. lo-cal. mayo lettuce 6 oz. can tomato juice	½ serving *Welsh Rarebit on 1 rusk or toast raw vegetables 1 c. skim milk	*Brunch* *Baked French Toast 1 tsp. margarine 1 tsp. brown sugar ½ c. fresh fruit cup, no sugar 1 T. *Fresh Fruit Topping 1 c. skim milk
Snack	1 small orange	½ pear	1 small nectarine	1 sm. orange	½ pear	sm. bunch grapes	¼ honeydew melon
Dinner	*Hawaiian Chicken 1 c. cooked rice asparagus spears tossed green salad lo-cal. dressing 1 c. skim milk	*Crisp Sesame Fillets 1 medium baked potato ⅓ c. peas deli coleslaw 1 c. skim milk	*Pasta Primevera lettuce wedge with lo-cal. dressing *orange custard 1 c. skim milk	*Italian Pork Chop Bake ½ c. green beans tossed green salad diet salad dressing 1 c. skim milk	*Quick Dinner:* 3 oz. (90 g) broiled lean ground beef burger, ketchup, mustard, relish on a wh. wheat bun ½ corn on the cob ½ tsp. margarine raw vegetables	*Dinner Party:* *Clam-Stuffed Mushrooms *Fiery Lamb Broil ½ c. *Couscous broccoli spears lemon wedges *Cocoa Roll or 1 glass wine	*Barley Burger Stew raw vegetables 1 c. skim milk nectarine
Snack	1 sm. apple	1 sm. orange	½ pear	1 sm. apple	½ c. fresh fruit cup 1 c. skim milk	½ c. fresh fruit cup 1 c. skim milk	1½ c. popped corn no butter
	Carbohydrate: 61% Total Fat: 20% Saturated Fat: 5%	Carbohydrate: 56% Total Fat: 23% Saturated Fat 5%	Carbohydrate: 62% Total Fat: 20% Saturated Fat: 5%	Carbohydrate: 56% Total Fat: 22% Saturated Fat: 8%	Carbohydrate: 53% Total Fat: 19% Saturated Fat: 5%	Carbohydrate: 46% Total Fat: 29% Saturated Fat: 10%	Carbohydrate: 59% Total Fat: 20% Saturated Fat: 7%

*Recipes included in the Recipe Section

1200 CALORIE MENU — WEEK #2

	Day 1	Day 2	Day 3	Day 4	Day 5	Day 6	Day 7
Breakfast	½ c. orange jce. ½ c. cooked cereal artificial sweetener 1 c. skim milk	½ c. grapefruit jce. 1½ c. cold cereal artificial sweetener 1 c. skim milk	½ c. blueberries ¾ c. cold cereal artificial sweetener 1 c. skim milk	½ c. orange jce. ½ wh. bagel 2 tsp. lt. cream cheese ½ T. diet jam 1 c. skim milk	½ c. grapefruit jce. ¾ c. cold cereal 1 c. skim milk	½ c. apple jce. *1 Whole Wheat Scone ½ T. diet jam 1 c. skim milk	*Quick Breakfast Before Exercise* ½ c. orange jce. *1 Whole Wheat Scone ½ T. diet jam 1 c. skim milk
Snack	2 oz. (60 g) lean ham on a kaiser roll with lettuce, tomato 1 T. lo-cal. mayo	*Snack Bar Lunch* 2 oz. (60 g) lean roast beef on wh. wh. bread, lettuce, tomato, mustard no spread on bread	½ c. leftover *Chili Bean Salad sm. roll raw vegetables 1 bunch grapes	*Lunch Out* French onion soup au gratin fresh fruit cup	½ c. low-fat cottage cheese 2 sl. pineapple 1 sm. roll 1 tsp. margarine	½ serving *Chick-Pea Soup raw vegetables ½ sl. wh. wh. bread	*Brunch* *1 Egg Benedict-Style 1 rusk or toast ½ c. fresh fruit cup
Lunch	1 sm. orange	1 sm. apple	1 sm. orange	1 sm. apple	1 sm. orange	1 sm. brunch grapes	
Dinner	*Pasta with Vegetable Clam Sauce tossed salad diet salad dressing 1 wh. wh. roll 1 tsp. margarine 1 c. skim milk	*Chili Bean Salad raw vegetables 1 tortilla, toasted in oven 2 T. bottled salsa for dipping 1 c. skim milk	*Lemon chicken baked potato 1 T. lo-cal. sour cream *Steamed Zucchini & Tomatoes tossed salad with diet salad dressing 1 c. skim milk	*Curried Tuna 1 c. rice broccoli spears 1 c. skim milk	*Pork Stroganoff 1 c. fresh pasta asparagus spears salad with lo-cal. dressing	*Roast Turkey *cranberry sauce ½ sm. baked squash cinnamon and sweetener ½ c. mashed potato *Blueberry Grunt	*Potato Pie tossed green salad with 1 T. lo-cal. dressing 1 c. skim milk 1 sm. nectarine
Snack	1 sm. pear	¼ honeydew melon	*banana muffin	1 sm. nectarine	1 c. low-fat yogurt with fruit	1 c. skim milk	
	Carbohydrate: 64% Total Fat: 19% Saturated Fat: 5%	Carbohydrate: 57% Total Fat: 22% Saturated Fat: 9%	Carbohydrate: 59% Total Fat: 21% Saturated Fat: 6%	Carbohydrate: 56% Total Fat: 24% Saturated Fat: 9%	Carbohydrate: 62% Total Fat: 11% Saturated Fat: 5%	Carbohydrate: 62% Total Fat: 17% Saturated Fat: 3%	Carbohydrate: 52% Total Fat: 29% Saturated Fat: 11%

*Recipes included in the Recipe Section

1500 CALORIE MENU — WEEK #1

	Day 1	Day 2	Day 3	Day 4	Day 5	Day 6	Day 7
Breakfast	½ banana 2 sl. wh. toast 1 tsp. margarine 1 T. diet jam 1 c. skim milk	½ c. orange jce. 1½ c. cold cereal artificial sweetener 1 c. skim milk	½ c. apple jce. 1 wh. wh. bagel 1 T. cream cheese 1 T. regular jam 1 c. skim milk	½ banana 1½ c. cold cereal artifical sweetener 1 c. skim milk	½ c. orange jce. 2 sl. wh. wh. toast 1 poached egg 1 tsp. margarine ½ T. diet jam 1 c. skim milk	½ c. grapefruit jce. 2 pancakes 1 tsp. margarine ¼ c. syrup 1 c. skim milk	*Quick Breakfast Before Exercise* ½ c. orange jce. 2 sl. wh. wh. toast 2 tsp. margarine 1 T. diet jam 1 c. skim milk
Snack			½ banana	1 nectarine	1 sm. bunch grapes		
Lunch	sandwich: 2 sl. wh. wh. bread 2 T. peanut butter 1 T. jam raw vegetables	*Lunch Out* 1 sl. cheese and vegetable pizza tossed vegetable salad with lemon wedge	sandwich: 2 sl. wh. wh. bread 2 oz. (60 g) drained tuna with 1 T. lo-cal. mayo raw vegetables	kaiser roll with 1 oz. (30 g) lean ham 1 oz. (30 g) cheese lettuce, tomato 1 T. lo-cal. mayo	sandwich: 2 sl. wh. wh. bread 2 oz. (60 g) drained tuna 1 T. lo-cal mayo lettuce raw vegetables	½ serving *Welsh Rarebit on 1 rusk or toast raw vegetables ¼ honeydew melon 1 c. skim milk	*Brunch* ½ grapefruit *Baked French Toast 1 tsp. margarine 2 tsp. brown sugar ½ c. fresh fruit cup 1 T. *Fresh Fruit Topping
Snack	1 sm. orange	1 sm. apple	1 sm. pear	1 sm. orange	1 sm. pear		1 oz. lo-fat cheese ¼ honeydew melon
Dinner	*Hawaiian Chicken 1 c. cooked rice asparagus spears tossed salad with 1 T. oil & vinegar 1 c. skim milk	*Crisp Sesame Fillets 1 med. baked potato 1 tsp. margarine ⅓ c. peas deli coleslaw	*Pasta Primevera lettuce wedge 1 T. lo-cal. mayo 1 lge. wh. wh. roll *Orange Custard 1 c. skim milk	*Italian Pork Chop Bake ½ c. green beans tossed salad with 1 T. lo-cal. dressing 1 c. skim milk	3 oz. (90 g) hamburger made with lean ground beef on a wh. wh. bun, ketchup, mustard, relish ½ c. corn on the cob ½ c. fresh fruit cup 1 c. skim milk	*Dinner Party* *Mushroom Caps with Clam Stuffing *Fiery Lamb Broil ½ c. *Couscous broccoli spears 1 sl. French bread OR 1 glass wine *Cocoa Roll	*Barley Burger Stew raw vegetables 1 wh. wh. roll 1 ts. margarine
Snack	1 *Cocoa Snackin' Cake	1 c. fruit lo-fat yogurt	1 nectarine	4 saltine crackers 1 T. jam	1½ c. popcorn 1 tsp. margarine		1½ c. popcorn 1 tsp. margarine
	Carbohydrate: 56% Total Fat: 28% Saturated Fat: 5%	Carbohydrate: 59% Total Fat: 23% Saturated Fat: 5%	Carbohydrate: 66% Total Fat: 19% Saturated Fat: 5%	Carbohydrate: 53% Total Fat: 28% Saturated Fat: 10%	Carbohydrate: 58% Total Fat: 21% Saturated Fat: 5%	Carbohydrate: 52% Total Fat: 29% Saturated Fat: 8%	Carbohydrate: 56% Total Fat: 28% Saturated Fat: 9%

*Recipes included in the Recipe Section

1500 CALORIE MENU — WEEK #2

	Day 1	Day 2	Day 3	Day 4	Day 5	Day 6	Day 7
Breakfast	½ c. orange jce. ½ c. cooked cereal 1 tsp. brown sugar 1 c. skim milk	½ c. grapefruit jce. 1 English muffin 1 tsp. margarine 1 T. jam 1 c. skim milk	½ c. blueberries 1½ c. cold cereal 1 c. skim milk	½ c. orange jce. 1 wh. wh. bagel 1 T. lt. cr. cheese 1 T. jam 1 c. skim milk	½ c. grapefruit jce. ¾ c. cold cereal ½ banana 1 c. skim milk	½ c. apple jce. 1 scrambled egg 1 *Whole Wheat Scone 1 tsp. jam 1 c. skim milk	*Quick Breakfast Before Exercise* ½ c. orange jce. 1 *Whole Wheat Scone 1 tsp. jam 1 c. skim milk
Snack			½ banana		2 *Oatmeal Buttons		
Lunch	2 oz. (60 g) lean ham on kaiser roll, lettuce, tomato 1 T. mayonnaise raw vegetables	*Snack/Bar Lunch* 2 oz. (60 g) lean roast beef on a wh. wh. roll lettuce, tomato, mustard, mayonnaise	1 serving leftover *Chili Bean Salad wh. wh. roll 1 tsp. margarine raw vegetables	*Lunch Out* French onion soup au gratin tossed salad with lemon ½ c. fresh fruit cup	½ c. lo-fat cottage cheese 2 sl. unsweetened pineapple 2 sm. wh. rolls 1 tsp. margarine	⅔ c. *Chick-pea Vegetable Soup raw vegetables	*Brunch* *Egg Benedict-Style 1 rusk or toast ½ c. fresh fruit cup
Snack	1 sm. orange	1 sm. apple	1 sm. orange		1 sm. orange	sm. bunch grapes	1 med. banana
Dinner	*Pasta with Vegetable Clam Sauce 1 wh. wh. roll tossed green salad with 1 T. oil & vinegar dressing	*Chili Bean Salad 2 tortillas, oven toasted ¼ c. salsa for dipping raw vegetables	*Lemon Chicken med. baked potato 1 T. lo-cal. sr. cream *Steamed Zucchini & Tomatoes salad with 1 T. Italian dressing	*Curried Tuna 1 c. rice broccoli florets ½ tsp. margarine nectarine	*Pork Stroganoff 1 c. cooked pasta asparagus spears tossed vegetable salad 1 T. salad dressing	*Roast Turkey Breast *Cranberry & Onion Sauce baked squash with 1 tsp. brown sugar ½ c. mashed potatoes 1 tsp. margarine *Blueberry Grunt *2 T. Fresh Fruit Topping	*Pie Plate Potato Pizza tossed vegetable salad 1 T. salad dressing 1 nectarine
Snack	5 soda crackers ½ T. peanut butter 1 c. skim milk	2 *Oatmeal Buttons 1 c. skim milk	1 *Banana Muffin 1 tsp. margarine 1 c. skim milk	1 sl. *Lemon Loaf 1 c. skim milk	1 c. lo-fat fruit yogurt	1 c. skim milk	2 *Oatmeal Buttons 1 c. skim milk
	Carbohydrate: 53% Total Fat: 28% Saturated Fat: .5%	Carbohydrate: 51% Total Fat: 30% Saturated Fat: 9%	Carbohydrate: 56% Total Fat: 26% Saturated Fat: 7%	Carbohydrate: 58% Total Fat: 25% Saturated Fat: 8%	Carbohydrate: 62% Total Fat: 17% Saturated Fat: 4%	Carbohydrate: 55% Total Fat: 22% Saturated Fat: 6%	Carbohydrate: 55% Total Fat: 30% Saturated Fat: 10%

*Recipes included in the Recipe Section

2000 CALORIE MENU — WEEK #1

	Day 1	Day 2	Day 3	Day 4	Day 5	Day 6	Day 7
Breakfast	1 med. banana 2 sl. wh. toast 2 tsp. margarine 1 T. honey or jam 1 c. 2% milk	½ c. orange jce. ½ c. blueberries 1½ c. cold cereal 1 tsp. sugar 1 c. 2% milk	½ c. apple jce. 1 wh. wh. bagel 2 T. cream cheese 1 T. jam 1 c. 2% milk	½ c. orange jce. 1½ c. cold cereal 1 banana 1 tsp. sugar 1 c. 2% milk	½ c. orange jce. 2 sl. wh. wh. toasts 1 poached egg 1 tsp. jam 1 c. 2% milk	½ c. apple jce. 3 pancakes 1 tsp. margarine ¼ c. syrup 1 c. 2% milk	*Quick Breakfast Before Exercise* 1 c. orange jce. 2 sl. wh. toast 2 tsp. margarine 1 T. jam 1 c. 2% milk
Snack	1 *Apricot Oatmeal Muffin	lge. bunch grapes	1 banana	apple	grapes	orange	—
Lunch	sandwich: 2 sl. wh. wh. bread, 2 T. peanut butter 1 T. jam or jelly raw vegetables 1 sm. orange 1 c. 2% milk	*Lunch Out* 2 sl. cheese & vegetable pizza salad with 1 T. oil & vinegar dressing 1 c. 2% milk	sandwich: 2 sl. wh. wh. bread, 2 oz. (60 g) tuna, 1 T. mayo, lettuce raw vegetables 1 c. 2% milk	kaiser roll with 1 oz. (30g) ham & cheese, lettuce, tomato mustard, 1 T. mayonnaise 1 c. 2% milk	sandwich: 2 sl. wh. wh. bread with 2 oz. (60 g) tuna, 1 T. mayo, lettuce raw vegetables 1 c. 2% milk	*Quick Lunch* *Welsh Rarebit on 2 Rusk or 2 toast raw vegetables ¼ honeydew melon 1 c. 2% milk	*Brunch* ½ grapefruit *Baked French Toast 2 tsp. margarine 1 T. brown sugar ½ c. fresh fruit cup 2 T. *Fresh Fruit Topping 1 c. 2% milk
Snack	1 apple	1 orange	1 pear	orange	pear	grapes	¼ honeydew melon
Dinner	*Hawaiian Chicken 1½ c. rice asparagus spears tossed vegetable salad 1 T. Italian dressing	*Crisp Sesame Fillets lg. baked potato peas deli coleslaw	*Pasta Primavera 1 wh. wh. roll 1 tsp. margarine lettuce wedge with 1 T. *Basic Dressing *Orange Custard	*Italian Pork Chop Bake green beans tossed green salad with 1 T. *Basic Dressing 1 s. wh. wh. bread	3 oz. (90 g) hamburger, made from lean ground beef, on a wh. wh. bun, ketchup, relish, mustard 1 cob of corn + 1 tsp. marg. ½ c. delicatessen coleslaw ½ c. fresh fruit cup	*Dinner Party* *Mushroom Caps with Clam Stuffing *Fiery Lamb Broil *Couscous broccoli spears *Caesar Salad** *Cocoa Roll filled with fresh fruit	*Lazy Sunday Supper* *Barley Burger Stew 1 wh. wh. roll 1 tsp. margarine raw vegetables
Snack	1 *Cocoa Snackin' Cake	1 c. lo-fat fruit yogurt	nectarine	*Apricot Oatmeal Muffin 1 T. jam or jelly	3 c. popcorn with 1 tsp. marg. apple	—	3 c. popcorn 1 T. margarine
	Carbohydrate: 57% Total Fat: 30% Saturated Fat: 6%	Carbohydrate: 55% Total Fat: 30% Saturated Fat: 7%	Carbohydrate: 56% Total Fat: 30% Saturated Fat: 9%	Carbohydrate: 53% Total Fat: 32% Saturated Fat: 9%	Carbohydrate: 54% Total Fat: 28% Saturated Fat: 8%	Carbohydrate: 53% Total Fat: 31% Saturated Fat: 11%	Carbohydrate: 58% Total Fat: 28% Saturated Fat: 9%

*Recipes included in the Recipe Section

2000 CALORIE MENU — WEEK #2

	Day 1	Day 2	Day 3	Day 4	Day 5	Day 6	Day 7
Breakfast	1 c. of orange jce. 1 c. cooked cereal 1 tsp. brown sugar 1 c. 2% milk	1 c. grapefruit jce. 1½ c. cold cereal ½ English muffin 1 tsp. margarine 1 tsp. honey or jam 1 c. 2% milk	1 c. apple jce. 1½ c. cold cereal ½ c. blueberries 1 tsp. sugar 1 c. 2% milk	1 c. orange jce. 2 wh. toast 2 tsp. margarine 1 T. jam 1 c. 2% milk	½ c. grapefruit jce. 1½ c. cold cereal ½ banana 1 tsp. sugar 2 sl. wh. wh. toast 2 tsp. margarine 1 T. jam 1 c. 2% milk	½ c. apple jce. 1 scrambled egg 2 *Whole Wheat Scones 1 tsp. margarine 1 c. 2% milk	*Quick Breakfast Before Exercise* 1 c. orange jce. 2 *Whole Wheat Scones 1 T. jam 1 c. 2% milk
Snack	*Banana Muffin	banana	grapes	*Banana Muffin	2 *Oatmeal Buttons	orange	
Lunch	kraiser roll with 1 oz. (30 g) ham and 1 oz. (30 g) cheese lettuce, tomato, 1 T. mayo 1 c. 2% milk	*Snack/Bar Lunch* 2 oz. (60 g) lean roast beef on a wh. wh. bun lettuce, tomato, mayo apple 1 c. 2% milk	left over *Chili Bean Salad 1 lge. wh. wh. roll 1 tsp. margarine raw vegetables 1 c. 2% milk	*Lunch Out* French onion soup 1 wh. wh. roll Salad with 1 T. French dressing 1 c. 2% milk	½ c. 2% cottage cheese 2 sl. canned pineapple lge. wh. wh. roll 2 tsp. margarine	¾ c. *Chick-Pea & Vegetable Soup sm. wh. wh. roll 1 tsp. margarine	*Brunch* *Egg Benedict-Style 2 rusk or toast ½ c. fresh fruit cup
Snack	orange		orange	apple	orange *Apricot Oatmeal Muffin	grapes	banana
Dinner	*Pasta with Vegetable Clam Sauce wh. wh. roll 1 tsp. margarine tossed green salad 1 T. Italian dressing	*Chili Bean Salad 3 tortillas, oven toasted salsa for dipping raw vegetables	*Lemon Chicken lge. baked potato 2 T. sour cream *Steamed Zucchini & Tomatoes tossed salad with 1 T. dressing	*Curried Tuna 1½ c. cooked rice broccoli florets nectarine	*Pork Stroganoff 1 c. cooked pasta asparagus spears ½ tsp. margarine	*Roast Turkey *Cranberry & Onion Sauce baked squash with 1 tsp. margarine & 2 tsp. brown sugar 1 c. mashed potatoes *Blueberry Grunt 2 T. Fresh Fruit Top	*Pie Plate Potato Pizza Tossed vegetable salad with 1 T. dressing nectarine
Snack	5 soda crackers 1 T. jelly	2 *Oatmeal Buttons 1 c. 2% milk	1 *Banana Muffin 1 tsp. margarine	½ c. lo-fat fruit yogurt	*Lemon Loaf 1 c. 2% milk	2 graham crackers 1 c. 2% milk	4 *Oatmeal Buttons 1 c. 2% milk
	Carbohydrate: 54% Total Fat: 30% Saturated Fat: 10%	Carbohydrate: 55% Total Fat: 30% Saturated Fat: 11%	Carbohydrate: 57% Total Fat: 29% Saturated Fat: 9%	Carbohydrate: 54% Total Fat: 30% Saturated Fat: 10%	Carbohydrate: 59% Total Fat: 24% Saturated Fat: 8%	Carbohydrate: 55% Total Fat: 29% Saturated Fat: 8%	Carbohydrate: 57% Total Fat: 30% Saturated Fat: 9%

*Recipes included in the Recipe Section

SAMPLE MENU LEGEND

For the sake of space, the following abbreviations have been used.

c. = cup
jce. = juice
g = grams
lge. = large
lt. = light
lo-cal. mayo = calorie-reduced mayonnaise-type dressing
marg. or margarine = soft, oil product with a polyunsaturated:
saturated fat ratio of 2:1 or better.
med. = medium
oz. = ounces
sl. = slices
sm. = small
sr. cream = sour cream
T. = tablespoon
tsp. = teaspoon
wh. gr. = whole grain
wh.wh. = whole-wheat
* indicated recipes are in the recipe section.
** there is a light version of this Caesar Salad in "Eat Light & Love It!", which will lower the fat content slightly.

Brunch, Lunch & Appetizers

BREAKFAST QUICHE

CRUST:

⅓ cup	all-purpose flour	75 mL
2 tbsp.	cornmeal	30 mL
2 tbsp.	water	30 mL
1 tbsp.	cooking oil	15 mL

FILLING:

¼ cup	thinly sliced onion	60 mL
1	egg, slightly beaten	1
½ cup	skim milk	125 mL
¼ tsp.	Worcestershire sauce	1 mL
4 drops	hot pepper sauce	4 drops
1 oz.	sharp cheese, grated	30 g
1 oz.	crab meat, real or mock	30 g
1 tbsp.	minced red pepper	15 mL

Combine crust ingredients. Mix with fork and gather into a ball. Divide the dough into 2 portions. Press 1 portion onto bottom and sides of a 1¼ cup (300 mL) custard cup, sprayed with nonstick spray. Repeat with the second portion of dough and a second custard cup. Bake at 400°F(200°C) 3-5 minutes or until pastry is dry and flaky. Combine the onion with a bit of water in a saucepan and simmer gently, just until softened. Drain. Combine egg and milk with seasonings. Layer ½ the onion, cheese, crab meat and red pepper in each crust. Pour half the egg mixture into each. Bake in 325°F(160°C) oven for 30 minutes, or until egg is set.

BREAKFAST QUICHE (Cont'd.)

MICROWAVE INSTRUCTIONS:

Prepare crust as above. Place on a rack to elevate and microwave on **high** for 3-4 minutes, rotating and pricking any bubbles with a fork after 2 minutes. Combine onion with a bit of water and microwave on **high** 1 minute to soften. Drain. Combine egg and milk with seasonings. Layer ½ the onion, cheese, crab meat and red pepper in each crust. Pour half the egg mixture into each. Place in microwave on a rack and microwave on **medium** 4-6 minutes, rotating at ½ time, until edges are set but center is just slightly soft and still shiny. Cover and allow to stand for 3-5 minutes. That will cook the center.

Yield: 2 servings

1 Serving

		Food Groups
Calories	317	2 R Meat
Protein	15 g	2 Bread
Total Fat	15 g	1 Fat
Saturated Fat	4 g	
Carbohydrate	30 g	
Cholesterol	133 mg	
Sodium	313 mg	

Serving Suggestion: As this is quite filling, a fruit salad would make the meal complete.

EGGS BENEDICT STYLE

2	eggs	2
2	slices toast OR 1 English muffin, split and toasted	2
½ cup	Benedict Sauce, page 43	125 mL

Poach the eggs as you always do, while the bread or muffin halves are toasting. Heat the sauce in a double boiler over hot water. Carefully place the egg on the toast. Put ¼ cup (60 mL) of the sauce on top.

MICROWAVE INSTRUCTIONS:

The sauce may be reheated in a glass measure on **low** for 2 minutes, stirring every 30 seconds.

Yield: 2 servings

1 Serving

Calories	259	**Food Groups**
Protein	18 g	2 R Meat
Total Fat	13 g	1 Bread
Saturated Fat	6 g	
Carbohydrate	18 g	
Cholesterol	222 mg	
Sodium	806 mg	

Serving Suggestion: What a marvelous brunch! And at half the calories and fat of 'the other' Eggs Benedict! You know, the one with Hollandaise.

BENEDICT SAUCE

½ cup	skim milk	125 mL
1 tbsp.	all-purpose flour	15 mL
⅛ tsp.	white pepper	0.5 mL
3-4 drops	hot pepper sauce	3-4 drops
¼ tsp.	Worcestershire sauce	1 mL
2 oz.	Swiss cheese, grated	60 g
2 oz.	skim milk cheese, grated	60 g
1 oz.	lean ham, slivered or minced	30 g

In a container with a tight lid, combine the skim milk and flour. Shake well to dissolve the flour. Pour into a heavy saucepan and stir over low heat until thickened and smooth. Add all of the remaining ingredients in order, except the ham, continuing to stir until the cheeses are melted and incorporated. Stir in the ham.

MICROWAVE INSTRUCTIONS:

In a container with a tight lid, combine the skim milk and flour. Shake well to dissolve the flour. Pour into a 2-cup (500 mL) glass measure. Microwave on **high** for 2 minutes, stirring every 30 seconds to prevent lumps. Add remaining ingredients in order, except the ham, continuing to stir until the cheeses are melted and incorporated. It may require another 30-45 seconds on **high** to melt the cheese. Stir in the ham.

Yield: 4 servings of ¼ cup (60 mL) each

1 Serving		
Calories	110	Food Groups
Protein	9 g	1 R Meat
Total Fat	6 g	½ Milk
Saturated Fat	3 g	
Carbohydrate	5 g	
Cholesterol	35 mg	
Sodium	625 mg	

Serving Suggestions: This sauce is used for the Eggs Benedict Style, page 42. It may also be used directly on toast, English muffins etc. as a quick hot breakfast item or on a baked potato for lunch. Try it!

BAKED FRENCH TOAST

2	egg whites	2
1	egg yolk	1
2 tsp.	grated orange rind	10 mL
1 cup	skim milk	250 mL
½ tsp.	vanilla extract	2 mL
4 slices	½" (1.3 cm) thick French bread	4 slices

The night before: Beat egg whites until stiff. Whisk together egg yolk, orange rind, milk and vanilla. Gently fold in egg whites. Pour ¼ of the egg mixture into a shallow baking pan. Lay the bread slices in a single layer in the egg mixture in the pan. Cover all bread slices evenly with the remaining egg mixture. Cover with plastic wrap and refrigerate overnight. In the morning: Heat the oven to 400°F (200°C). Lightly brown each slice of bread in a frying pan sprayed with nonstick spray. Then place the slices on a baking sheet and bake in the oven until each slice has puffed in the center, approximately 10-12 minutes. Serve immediately.

MICROWAVE INTRUCTIONS:

Follow the instructions above for the night before. In the morning, lightly brown each slice in a frying pan sprayed with nonstick spray. Place in a microwave baking dish and microwave at **medium** for 3 minutes, or until puffed in the center. Serve immediately.

Yield: 2 servings

1 Serving

Calories	222	**Food Groups**
Protein	15 g	2 L Meat
Total Fat	4 g	2 Bread
Saturated Fat	2 g	
Carbohydrate	29 g	
Cholesterol	154 mg	
Sodium	378 mg	

Tip: This is a good way to use up French bread that has become slightly dry. Serve with syrup, brown sugar or fresh fruit, depending upon how many calories you wish to add.

MINI SHRIMP PIZZAS

1 cup	tomato sauce	250 mL
4 oz.	can shrimp	113 g
1 tbsp.	olive oil	15 mL
¼ cup	minced onion	60 mL
½ cup	sliced mushrooms	125 mL
4 tbsp.	grated Parmesan cheese	60 mL
¼ tsp.	garlic powder	1 mL
¼ tsp.	crushed basil leaves	1 mL
¼ tsp.	crushed oregano leaves	1 mL
3	English muffins, split	3

Combine the first 9 ingredients in a bowl. Heap onto English muffin halves. Place on a baking sheet and bake in a 350°F(150°C) oven for 15 minutes, or until hot and bubbly. Serve at once.

MICROWAVE INSTRUCTIONS:

Prepare as above. Place on a rack in a baking dish and microwave on **high** 3-4 minutes, or until bubbly. Rotate at half time.

Yield: 2 servings

1 Serving

		Food Groups
Calories	399	
Protein	26 g	3 L Meat
Total Fat	14 g	2 ½ Bread
Saturated Fat	4 g	1 Vegetable
Carbohydrate	43 g	1 Fat
Cholesterol	95 mg	
Sodium	761 mg	

Serving Suggestion: As these are quite filling, a simple salad will probably be all one wants with them. To serve as appetizers, cut muffins into quarters.

HUMUS IN A PITA

This is a sandwich that will carry you through the afternoon!

1 cup	canned chick-peas, drained	250 mL
¼ tsp.	garlic powder	1 mL
¼ tsp.	salt (optional)	1 mL
¼ tsp.	black pepper	1 mL
1 tbsp.	chopped fresh parsley	15 mL
2 tsp.	olive oil	10 mL
8"	pita bread	20 cm
	chopped lettuce or alfalfa sprouts	
¼	small tomato, diced	¼
2 oz.	low-fat mozzarella cheese, grated	60 g

Place first 6 ingredients in blender or food processor and process until smooth. Cut pita bread in half and open the pockets. Spread the humus on the inside of each pita half. Combine the lettuce or sprouts, tomato and cheese. Heap in the center of each pita.

Yield: 2 servings

1 Serving

Calories	379	**Food Groups**	
Protein	18 g	2 R Meat	
Total Fat	13 g	3 Bread	
Saturated Fat	4 g	1 Fat	
Carbohydrate	47 g		
Cholesterol	23 mg		
Sodium	375 mg		

Serving Suggestion: Humus may be served alone as a dip, to be used with pita bread pieces or raw vegetables as dippers.

TUNA MELT

2	English muffins, split	2
6 ½ oz.	can solid tuna	184 g
¼ cup	minced celery	60 mL
1 tbsp.	minced green onion (optional)	15 mL
2 tbsp.	reduced-calorie mayonnaise	30 mL
2 tbsp.	low-fat yogurt	30 mL
2 slices	tomato	2 slices
2 oz.	low-fat mozzarella cheese	60 g

Split and toast English muffin halves. Combine tuna, celery onion, mayonnaise and yogurt. Divide and spread on the 4 muffin halves. Place a slice of tomato on each. Grate the cheese and top each muffin with ¼ of it. Place muffins on a baking sheet and bake in a 350°F (180°C) oven for 10 minutes, or until the cheese is melted and tuna is heated.

MICROWAVE INSTRUCTIONS:

Combine as above, but place on a rack in a shallow pan or on a paper towel, and microwave on **medium** 1 minute. Rotate and microwave on **medium** another minute, or until cheese is melted and tuna is heated.

Yield: 2 servings

1 Serving

Calories	356	Food Groups	
Protein	27 g	4 L Meat	
Total Fat	14 g	2 Bread	
Saturated Fat	5 g	1 Fat	
Carbohydrate	28 g		
Cholesterol	54 mg		
Sodium	799 mg		

Serving Suggestion: This is a busy night special. Just add a vegetable and fruit.

OPEN-FACED ROAST BEEF SANDWICH

A use for leftover roast beef.

4 oz.	French bread stick	120 g
2 tsp.	horseradish	10 mL
1 tbsp.	low-calorie mayonnaise	15 mL
1 tbsp.	low-fat yogurt	15 mL
4	1 oz. (30 g) slices lean roast beef	4
4 slices	tomato, large	4 slices
4	green pepper rings	4
2 slices	Spanish onion, separated into rings	2 slices
1.5 oz.	low-fat mozzarella cheese, shredded	45 g

Buy a French stick, weigh it. Score into 2 ounce (60 g) pieces. Cut off 2 ounces (60 g) for each sandwich. Split in half lengthwise. Lay on cookie sheet cut side up. Mix horseradish, low-calorie mayonnaise and yogurt. Spread on both sandwiches. Lay 1 slice of roast beef on each half of each sandwich. Layer the tomato, green pepper and Spanish onion. Sprinkle each sandwich with half the mozzarella cheese. Broil until cheese is melted. Serve immediately.

Yield: 2 servings

1 Serving

Calories	382	**Food Groups**	
Protein	29 g	3 R Meat	
Total Fat	12 g	2 Bread	
Saturated Fat	4 g	2 Vegetables	
Carbohydrate	39 g		
Cholesterol	67 mg		
Sodium	536 mg		

Serving Suggestion: A relish tray with raw vegetables, pickles, etc. goes nicely with these sandwiches.

See photograph opposite.

Open-Faced Roast Beef Sandwich, page 48

REUBEN SANDWICH

2 slices	rye bread	2 slices
2 tsp.	mustard	10 mL
2 oz.	lean pastrami	60 g
½ cup	sauerkraut, drained	125 mL
1 oz.	low-fat mozzarella cheese	30 g

Spread your favorite rye bread with your favorite mustard. On one slice place the pastrami, sauerkraut and the **low**-fat mozzarella cheese. Place on a cookie sheet in a 400°F (200°C) oven for 4 minutes, or until cheese is melted. Top with second slice of bread.

MICROWAVE INSTRUCTIONS:

Spread the rye bread with the mustard. On 1 slice place the pastrami, sauerkraut and the low-fat mozzarella cheese. Place on a microwave rack or on paper towel on a plate. Microwave on **high** for 1 minute to heat meat and sauerkraut and melt cheese. Rotate after 30 seconds. Top with second slice of bread.

Yield: 1 sandwich

1 Sandwich

		Food Groups
Calories	280	
Protein	23 g	3 L Meat
Total Fat	8 g	2 Bread
Saturated Fat	3 g	
Carbohydrate	31 g	
Cholesterol	53 mg	
Sodium	2104 mg	

Note: This **high** sodium meal probably should not be indulged in on a regular basis, but it certainly is a quick dinner for times when you are in a rush! Serve with coleslaw.

MUSHROOM CAPS WITH CLAM STUFFING

16 large	mushroom caps	16 large
½ cup	minced clams	125 mL
2 tsp.	soft margarine or butter	10 mL
¼ cup	minced mushroom stems	60 mL
1	green onion, minced	1
1	garlic clove, minced	1
⅛ tsp.	pepper	0.5 mL
1 tbsp.	minced parsley	15 mL
2 tbsp.	bread crumbs	30 mL

Wash and dry the mushroom caps. Place the minced clams in a bowl. Melt the margarine in a small frying pan and add the mushroom stems, onion, garlic and pepper. Saute just until the mushrooms are soft. Add this to the minced clams, along with the parsley and bread crumbs. Mix well with a fork. Mound filling by the teaspoonful (7-10 mL) on the mushroom caps. Place the caps on a rack in a baking dish and bake in a 400°F (200°C) oven for 10 minutes, or until the mushrooms are cooked. Remove them from the oven and arrange on serving plates or on a platter, if passing.

MICROWAVE INSTRUCTIONS:

Wash and dry the mushroom caps. Place the clams in a bowl. In a microwave dish, melt the margarine on **high** for 30 seconds. Add the mushroom stems, onion, garlic and pepper. Microwave on **high** for 2 minutes. Stir into the clams. Add the parsley and breadcrumbs. Mix well with a fork. Mound by the teaspoonful on the mushroom caps. Place the caps on a microwave rack in a baking dish and microwave on **high** for 5-6 minutes, or until the mushrooms are soft. Rotate at half time. Remove them from the oven and arrange on serving plates or on a platter, if passing.

Yield: 16 appetizers

MUSHROOM CAPS WITH CLAM STUFFING (Cont'd.)

1 Appetizer

Calories	18	**Food Groups**
Protein	1 g	1 Vegetable
Total Fat	1 g	
Saturated Fat	0 g	
Carbohydrate	2 g	
Cholesterol	4 mg	
Sodium	17 mg	

Serving Suggestion: For a dinner party, serve 4 to a plate, garnish with fresh parsley and a lemon wedge. If passing, allow mushrooms to stand a minute so they will be dry and not too hot to handle.

CLAM DIP

½ cup	canned clams	125 mL
1 tbsp.	clam juice	15 mL
¾ cup	light cream cheese	175 mL
3-4 drops	hot pepper sauce	3-4 drops
1 tbsp.	chopped parsley	15 mL
1	green onion, chopped	1
1 tsp.	lemon juice	5 mL
1	garlic clove, chopped	1

Combine all ingredients in blender jar. Cover and blend on medium speed until combined and smooth. Pour into serving container and chill thoroughly. Makes 1¼ cups (300 mL).

Yield: 20 servings of 1 tbsp. (15 mL) each

1 Serving

Calories	24	**Food Groups**
Protein	1 g	½ Fat
Total Fat	2 g	
Saturated Fat	0 g	
Carbohydrate	1 g	
Cholesterol	3 mg	
Sodium	6 mg	

Serving Suggestions: This dip is lovely with a variety of vegetables and also as a spread on crackers.

SPINACH DIP

We served this "defatted version" of a popular dip to the person who gave us the original "fat" version. She didn't notice the difference!

5 oz.	frozen chopped spinach	150 g
½ cup	low-fat sour cream	125 mL
½ cup	calorie-reduced mayonnaise	125 mL
½ env.	dehydrated vegetable soup mix	20 g
½ cup	low-fat yogurt	125 mL
1	green onion, minced	1

Thaw the spinach and put it in a sieve. Press the spinach against the bottom and sides with a spoon, to remove the excess water. Combine with sour cream, mayonnaise and soup mix. Mix well. Gently stir in yogurt and green onion. Refrigerate and let stand for 2 hours to allow flavors to blend.

Yield: 16 servings of 2 tbsp. (30 mL) each

1 Serving

Calories	42	**Food Groups**
Protein	1 g	½ Fat
Total Fat	3 g	1 Vegetable
Saturated Fat	1 g	
Carbohydrate	3 g	
Cholesterol	3 mg	
Sodium	163 mg	

Serving Suggestions: Purchase a round loaf of dark rye bread. Cut off the top, hollow it out by pulling the bread out in bite-sized pieces. Put bread pieces in a bowl and cover with a damp towel. When ready to serve, pour the dip into the hollow bread, and surround with the bread pieces, to be used for dipping. Bread may also be placed on a cookie sheet, wrapped in foil and baked at 300°F (150°C) for 1½ hours. Hot or cold dip is also wonderful with raw vegetable dippers.

TANGY CHEESE DIP

8 oz.	spreadable lite cream cheese	250 g
1 oz.	blue or Roquefort cheese	30 g
1 tsp.	grated fresh onion	5 mL
1 tsp.	Worcestershire sauce	5 mL

Place the cream cheese in a bowl. Crumble the blue or Roquefort cheese and add it, plus the onion and Worcestershire sauce, to the cream cheese. Mix well with a fork. Cover and refrigerate at least 1 hour.

Yield: 16 servings of 1 tbsp. (15 mL) each

1 Serving

Calories	38	**Food Groups**
Protein	1 g	1 Fat
Total Fat	3 g	
Saturated Fat	1 g	
Carbohydrate	1 g	
Cholesterol	1 mg	
Sodium	29 mg	

Serving Suggestion: Terrific as a dip for fresh vegetables, crackers, bread sticks or fill celery ribs and cut into bite-sized pieces.

WELSH RAREBIT

2 oz.	extra-old Cheddar cheese	60 g
3 oz.	skim milk cheese	90 g
¼ cup	beer	60 mL
¼ tsp.	dry mustard	1 mL
½ tsp.	Worcestershire sauce	2 mL
½ tsp.	paprika	2 mL
1	egg, slightly beaten	1

Combine all of the ingredients, except the egg, in a heavy saucepan. Cook over low heat until cheese is melted. Remove from heat. Slowly pour the egg into the cheese mixture, stirring as you pour. Return to heat for 1 minute, stirring constantly.

MICROWAVE INSTRUCTIONS:

Combine all of the ingredients, except the egg, in a 2 cup (500 mL) glass measure. Microwave on **low** for 2 minutes, or until cheese is melted. Stir once each minute. Slowly pour the egg into the cheese mixture, stirring as you pour. Microwave on **high** for 30 seconds, or until bubbles form. Stir well after 15 seconds.

Yield: 2 servings

1 Serving

Calories	247	Food Groups
Protein	21 g	3 R Meat
Total Fat	15 g	
Saturated Fat	9 g	
Carbohydrate	6 g	
Cholesterol	211 mg	
Sodium	859 mg	

Serving Suggestions: Serve on toast or rusk. If you like, place a slice of tomato on the toast, spoon the sauce over and place under the broiler for a minute, using an ovenproof plate, of course. For a new twist, use fondue forks to dip bread cubes or assorted fresh vegetables into hot Rarebit. Great as an appetizer or après ski, skating or theater treat.

Muffins & Breads

HAM AND CHEESE BREAKFAST MUFFIN

½ cup	skim milk	125 mL
2 tsp.	vinegar	10 mL
⅔ cup	all-purpose flour	150 mL
¼ cup	cornmeal	60 mL
½ tsp.	baking powder	2 mL
½ tsp.	baking soda	2 mL
1 oz.	lean cooked ham, chopped	30 g
1½ oz.	sharp cheese, grated	45 g
1	egg, lightly beaten	1
½ tbsp.	vegetable oil	7 mL

Combine milk and vinegar and set aside. Combine dry ingredients in a large bowl. Add ham and approximately ¾ of cheese. Mix with fork until ham is well dispersed. Combine egg, milk mixture and oil. Stir quickly into dry ingredients, mixing until just combined. Divide into 6 muffin cups that have been sprayed with a nonstick spray. Sprinkle remaining cheese on muffins. Bake at 400°F (200°C) for 15 minutes, or until golden done.

MICROWAVE INSTRUCTIONS:

Prepare as above, dividing into microwave muffin pan lined with paper baking cups. Microwave on **high** for 3-5 minutes. Rotate at half cooking time. Test for doneness.

Yield: 6 muffins

1 Muffin

Calories	149	Food Groups
Protein	6 g	1 R Meat
Fat	5 g	1 Bread
Saturated Fat	2 g	
Carbohydrate	18 g	
Cholesterol	45 mg	
Sodium	285 mg	

Note: Because of the ham, these muffins must be refrigerated and should be heated before serving.

APRICOT OATMEAL MUFFIN

½ cup	rolled oats	125 mL
½ cup	low-fat yogurt	125 mL
2 tbsp.	cooking oil	30 mL
½ cup	all-purpose flour	125 mL
1 tbsp.	granulated sugar	15 mL
1 tsp.	baking powder	5 mL
½ tsp.	baking soda	2 mL
⅛ tsp.	salt	0.5 mL
¼ cup	chopped, dried apricots	60 mL
1 tbsp.	chopped pecans or walnuts	15 mL
1 tbsp.	brown sugar	15 mL
½ tsp.	cinnamon	2 mL

Combine the oats, yogurt and oil in a bowl. Sift the flour, sugar, baking powder, soda and salt together. Add the dried apricots and nuts. Mix well to separate the apricots. Combine the dry and wet ingredients with a fork, just until wet. Distribute evenly among 6 muffin cups, sprayed with a nonstick spray. Combine brown sugar and cinnamon; sprinkle over muffins. Press gently with back of fork, so sugar doesn't roll off as muffins rise. Bake at 425°F (220°C) for 15 minutes.

MICROWAVE INSTRUCTIONS:

Prepare batter as above. Distribute among 6 microwave muffin cups lined with paper baking cups. Combine brown sugar and cinnamon and proceed as above. Microwave on **high** 3-5 minutes, rotating at ½ time. Test for doneness by inserting a toothpick in the center. It should come out clean.

Yield: 6 muffins

1 Muffin

Calories	165	**Food Groups**
Protein	4 g	1 Bread
Total Fat	7 g	½ Fruit
Saturated Fat	1 g	1 Fat
Carbohydrate	21 g	
Cholesterol	40 mg	
Sodium	180 mg	

Note: This is our highest calorie muffin, but very nourishing. Add fruit juice and a glass of milk for a quick breakfast.

Very Good!

BANANA MUFFINS

¾ cup	all-purpose flour	175 mL
½ cup	whole-wheat flour	125 mL
3 tbsp.	brown sugar	45 mL
1 tsp.	baking powder	5 mL
½ tsp.	baking soda	2 mL
¼ tsp.	salt	1 mL
2 tbsp.	chopped nuts MACADAMIA	30 mL
1	egg, slightly beaten	1
1½ ¾ cup	mashed banana 2 LARGE	175 mL
2 tbsp.	cooking oil	30 mL
2 tbsp.	orange juice	30 mL

In a large bowl, combine all of the dry ingredients. Combine the egg, banana, oil and orange juice. Mix well. Stir into the dry ingredients until just moistened. Turn into a muffin pan that has been sprayed with a nonstick spray. Bake at 375°F (190°C) for 15 minutes, or until done. *USE 6/MUFFIN PAN - FILL TO*
18min   *BRIM + USE 1C MEASURING CUP*
FOR BALANCE

MICROWAVE INSTRUCTIONS:

In a medium bowl, combine all of the dry ingredients. Combine the egg, banana, oil and orange juice. Mix well. Stir into the dry ingredients until just moistened. Turn into a microwave muffin pan that has been lined with paper baking cups. Microwave in 2 batches. Microwave on **high** 3-5 minutes per batch, or just until the muffins lose their batter-like appearance. Rotate at halftime.

Yield: 10 muffins

1 Muffin

Calories	135	Food Groups
Protein	3 g	1½ Bread
Total Fat	4 g	1 Fat
Saturated Fat	0 g	
Carbohydrate	22 g	
Cholesterol	24 mg	
Sodium	153 mg	

WHOLE-WHEAT SCONES

1¼ cups	whole-wheat flour	300 mL
2 tsp.	baking powder	10 mL
¼ tsp.	salt	1 mL
¼ cup	sugar	60 mL
¼ cup	cooking oil	60 mL
½ cup	skim milk	125 mL
¼ cup	currants	60 mL

In a medium bowl combine dry ingredients, except currants. Combine oil and milk, and whisk a bit with a fork. Add currants and pour all at once into flour mixture. Mix gently with a fork until just moistened. Pat into a pie pan that has been sprayed with a nonstick spray. Bake at 450°F (220°C) for 10 minutes. Cut into 8 wedges and serve hot.

MICROWAVE INSTRUCTIONS:

Prepare as above. Microwave on **high** for 4-6 minutes, rotating at ½ time, and test for doneness with a toothpick at 4 minutes.

Yield: 8 servings

1 Serving

		Food Groups	
Calories	196	Food Groups	
Protein	3 g	1⅓ Bread	
Total Fat	8 g	1½ Fat	
Saturated Fat	0 g	2 tsp. sugar	
Carbohydrate	30 g		
Cholesterol	0 mg		
Sodium	74 mg		

Note: While higher in fat than most of our recipes, none of the fat is saturated so this is a nice treat for the person on a cholesterol-lowering diet, as long as the total fat for the day stays within 30% of calories.

EASY CINNAMON BUNS

1 loaf	*frozen bread dough	1 loaf
2 tbsp.	melted margarine or butter	30 mL
2 tsp.	ground cinnamon	10 mL
1 tbsp.	brown sugar	15 mL

*Quick thaw: Place frozen loaf in a microwave-safe loaf pan that has been sprayed with a nonstick spray. Microwave on **low** for 3½ to 5 minutes or until just slightly firm in the center. Let stand for 10-15 minutes.

Allow the dough to thaw completely, but do not allow it to rise. On a floured board, roll out to a rectangle approximately 10 x 16" (24 x 40 cm). Spread with 1 tbsp. (15 mL) margarine. Sprinkle with cinnamon and brown sugar. Roll the dough up towards you, starting at the long edge. Keep the roll as tight as possible. Seal the final seam by pinching it closed. Slice the roll into 16 slices and place them on a baking sheet that has been sprayed with a nonstick spray. Allow to rise in a warm place until almost double. Brush tops and sides with remaining margarine. Bake in a preheated 425°F (210°C) oven for 15 minutes, until slightly browned. Cool slightly; remove.

MICROWAVE INSTRUCTIONS:

Prepare as above. Place the sliced buns on 2 glass pie plates, that have been sprayed with a nonstick spray. Leave the middle empty, placing the buns around the edge. Allow to rise in a warm place, covered, until almost double in size. Brush tops and sides with the remaining melted margarine. Microwave on **medium** for 6-8 minutes, rotating every 2 minutes.

Yield: 16 buns

1 Bun

Calories	79		Food Groups
Protein	2 g		1 Bread
Total Fat	2 g		
Saturated Fat	0 g		
Carbohydrate	13 g		
Cholesterol	1 mg		
Sodium	135 mg		

Note: These will freeze well. Warm before serving.

RICH BRAN BREAD

1¼ cups	whole-wheat flour	300 mL
1 cup	all-purpose flour	250 mL
½ cup	brown sugar	125 mL
3 tsp.	baking powder	15 mL
½ cup	raisins	125 mL
2	eggs, slightly beaten	2
1¼ cups	skim milk	300 mL
1½ cups	whole-bran cereal	375 mL
2 tbsp.	molasses	30 mL
2 tbsp.	cooking oil	30 mL

Spray a 5 x 9" (13 x 23 cm) loaf pan with nonstick spray. Preheat oven to 350°F (180°C). In a medium bowl, combine all of the dry ingredients. In another bowl beat eggs, add the milk, cereal, molasses and oil. Allow to stand for 3 minutes to soften bran. Pour milk mixture into dry ingredients and mix with a fork until just moistened. Pour into prepared pan and bake for 50 minutes. Let stand for 10 minutes before removing from pan. When cooled, wrap tightly and refrigerate or freeze.

MICROWAVE INSTRUCTIONS:

Combine as above. Pour batter into a microwave bundt pan that has been sprayed with nonstick spray. Microwave on **medium** 11-13 minutes, or until toothpick inserted in the center comes out clean. Let stand on a rack for 10 minutes before removing from pan. When cooled, wrap tightly and store in refrigerator or freezer.

Yield: 16 slices

1 Slice

		Food Groups
Calories	162	
Protein	4 g	1½ Bread
Total Fat	3 g	½ Fat
Saturated Fat	0 g	2 tsp. sugar
Carbohydrate	32 g	
Cholesterol	30 mg	
Sodium	74 mg	

Serving Suggestion: This is tasty for breakfast, coffee break or as an evening snack. Just warm a bit and serve.

Good!

WHOLE-GRAIN SODA BREAD

1 cup	all-purpose flour	250 mL
2 tbsp.	brown sugar	30 mL
1 tsp.	baking powder	5 mL
1 tsp.	baking soda	5 mL
½ tsp.	salt	2 mL
2 tbsp.	soft margarine or butter	30 mL
2 cups	whole-wheat flour	500 mL
¼ cup	rolled oats	60 mL
1½ cups	buttermilk	375 mL
	margarine for glaze	

Combine first 5 ingredients in a large bowl. Cut in the margarine with 2 knives or a pastry blender. Stir in the whole-wheat flour and the oats. Make a well in the center and pour in the buttermilk. Stir well. Turn out onto a floured board and knead 1 minute only. Shape into a ball and place on a greased baking sheet. Score the top with a wet knife blade. Bake in a 375°F (190°C) oven for 35-40 minutes. Remove to cooling rack and brush top with a bit of melted margarine.

Yield: 16 servings

1 Serving

Calories	114	Food Groups
Protein	4 g	1½ Bread
Total Fat	2 g	½ Fat
Saturated Fat	0 g	
Carbohydrate	21 g	
Cholesterol	0 mg	
Sodium	212 mg	

Note: This is a great bread for the person who really isn't into bread baking but once in awhile would love to have really fresh bread, with a minimum of effort!

See photograph page 64A.

Soups

BEEF, BARLEY, BEAN SOUP

6 oz.	flank steak, bite-sized pieces	170 g
3 cups	beef bouillon or broth	750 mL
2 tbsp.	pot or pearl barley	30 mL
1 cup	chopped onion	250 mL
½ cup	crushed, canned tomatoes	125 mL
1	garlic clove, minced	1
¼ cup	chopped green pepper	60 mL
¼ cup	sliced carrots	60 mL
1 cup	frozen baby lima beans	250 mL
½ tsp.	thyme	2 mL
¼ tsp.	cumin	1 mL
1	celery stalk, sliced thinly	1
1	small parsnip, julienne strips	1

Combine steak, bouillon, barley, onion, tomatoes and garlic in a heavy cooking pot with lid. Simmer, covered, for 1-2 hours, or until meat is tender. Add green pepper, carrots, lima beans, thyme and cumin. Cook another 15 minutes. Add celery and parsnip and cook about 10 minutes more.

MICROWAVE INSTRUCTIONS:

Combine steak, bouillon, barley, onion, tomatoes and garlic in a large microwave casserole with a lid. Cover; microwave on **high** 15 minutes. Stir; cook on medium 15 minutes more. Add green pepper, carrots, lima beans, thyme and cumin. Microwave on **high** 7 minutes. Add celery and parsnips, microwave on **high** 5 minutes, until vegetables are **just** tender.

Yield: 2 servings

1 Serving

		Food Groups
Calories	402	
Protein	30 g	4 L Meat
Total Fat	12 g	2 Bread
Saturated Fat	5 g	2 Vegetables
Carbohydrates	44 g	
Cholesterol	68 mg	
Sodium	1592 mg	

Serving Suggestion: Serve with salad and whole-grain bread.

See photograph opposite.

Beef, Barley, Bean Soup, page 64
Whole-Grain Soda Bread, page 62

TUNA CORN CHOWDER

1 cup	skim milk	250 mL
¼ cup	chopped onion	60 mL
1	celery stalk, sliced	1
1	medium potato, diced	1
¼ tsp.	ground summer savory	1 mL
⅛ tsp	pepper	0.5 mL
½ cup	cream-style corn	125 mL
6 ½ oz.	can tuna, drained	184 g

In a medium saucepan, combine milk with onion, celery and potato. Cover and simmer until celery is softened, about 10 minutes. Stir in savory, pepper, corn and tuna, which has been broken into small chunks. Heat through and serve.

MICROWAVE INSTRUCTIONS:

In a deep container (at least 6-cup [1.5 L] capacity) or 6-cup casserole with lid, combine milk with onion, celery and potato. Cover and microwave on **medium** for 10 minutes, stirring twice, or until celery is softened. Stir in savory, pepper, corn and tuna, which has been broken into small chunks. Microwave on **medium** 1 minute more to heat through. Serve at once.

Yield: 2 servings

1 Serving

		Food Groups
Calories	288	
Protein	28 g	4 L Meat
Total Fat	7 g	1½ Bread
Saturated Fat	1 g	1 Skim Milk
Carbohydrate	31 g	
Cholesterol	49 mg	
Sodium	854 mg	

Serving Suggestion: Accompany this with a green salad and a slice of French bread.

CREAM OF CRAB SOUP

2 tsp.	soft margarine or butter	10 mL
½ cup	diced celery	125 mL
½ cup	minced onion	125 mL
2 tbsp.	flour	30 mL
⅓ cup	skim milk powder	75 mL
1½ cups	skim milk	375 mL
⅛ tsp.	salt	0.5 mL
⅛ tsp.	white pepper	0.5 mL
3-4 drops	hot pepper sauce	3-4 drops
2 tbsp.	white wine	30 mL
6 oz.	crab meat or mock crab, shredded	180 g

In a heavy saucepan, melt the margarine. Add the celery and onion and sauté, at very low heat, for 10 minutes. You want to soften the vegetables but not brown them. Stir in the flour. Blend well. Add the skim milk powder to the skim milk and mix well. Gradually pour about ½ cup (125 mL) of the milk into the onion, flour mixture. Stir constantly until it thickens and there are no lumps of flour. Continue to stir and add remaining milk gradually, until it is all incorporated. Season with the salt, pepper, hot pepper sauce and wine. Heat, **below a boil**, for 3-4 minutes. Stir in the crab and heat through. Serve at once.

MICROWAVE INSTRUCTIONS:

In a deep microwave bowl, place margarine, celery and onion. Cover. Microwave on **high** 3-4 minutes, or until celery is soft. Remove from microwave and stir in flour. In a separate container, mix the skim milk powder into the skim milk and blend until smooth. Microwave on **high** 2 minutes, or until just below a boil. Gradually stir into onion-flour mixture, until thickened and there are no lumps of flour. Stir in remaining seasonings, wine and crab. Microwave on **low** 1-2 minutes just to heat through. Serve immediately.

Yield: 2 servings

1 Serving

Calories	253	Food Groups
Protein	23 g	3 L Meat
Total Fat	6 g	1 Bread
Saturated Fat	1 g	2 Milk
Carbohydrate	26 g	
Cholesterol	66 mg	
Sodium	464 mg	

Serving Suggestion: Serve with a vegetable salad and a piece of Whole-Grain Soda Bread, page 62, to make a great supper.

CHICK-PEA VEGETABLE SOUP

14 oz. can	chick-peas	390 mL
	juice from chickpeas	
½ cup	chopped onion	125 mL
½ cup	chopped green pepper	125 mL
½ cup	chopped celery	125 mL
1 cup	water	250 mL
1	garlic clove, minced	1
1	bay leaf	1
½	chicken bouillon cube OR ½ tsp. (2 mL) chicken base	½
½ tsp.	Worcestershire sauce	2 mL
⅛ tsp.	crushed basil leaves	0.5 mL
1 tbsp.	chopped fresh parsley	15 mL
½ cup	crushed, canned tomatoes	125 mL
2 oz.	part-skim mozzarella cheese, grated	60 g

In a large saucepan, combine the first 12 ingredients. Cover and bring to a boil. Reduce heat and simmer for 15 to 20 minutes. Stir in the tomatoes and reheat. Ladle into serving bowls. Sprinkle with grated cheese.

MICROWAVE INSTRUCTIONS:

Combine first 12 ingredients in a large casserole with lid. Microwave on **high** for 5 minutes. Reduce to **low** and simmer 10 minutes more, or until vegetables are cooked. Stir in tomatoes, reheat on **high** for 1 minute. Ladle into serving bowls and sprinkle with grated cheese.

Yield: 2 servings

1 Serving

		Food Groups
Calories	335	
Protein	20 g	3 L Meat
Total Fat	8 g	2 Bread
Saturated Fat	3 g	2 Vegetables
Carbohydrate	47 g	
Cholesterol	24 mg	
Sodium	508 mg	

CURRIED PEA SOUP

1	small leek	1
1 cup	chicken broth	250 mL
1	medium potato, peeled & diced	1
¼ tsp.	curry powder	1 mL
⅛ tsp.	white pepper	0.5 mL
½ cup	fresh or frozen peas	125 mL
¼ cup	low-fat yogurt	60 mL
2 tbsp.	skim milk	30 mL

Cut the bottom off the leek and remove any soft or discolored top parts. Slice the leek, using only about 2" (5 cm) of the green stalk, and wash well in a bowl or sink full of water. (Leeks are notoriously sandy so wash thoroughly.) Drain. Combine the leek, chicken broth and potato in a medium saucepan with a lid. Add the curry powder and pepper. Cover, bring to a boil and simmer for about 20 minutes, or until the leek and potato are cooked and soft. Add peas; cook 5 minutes. Allow to cool slightly. Place soup in blender. Blend until smooth. Refrigerate. Stir in yogurt and skim milk just before serving.

MICROWAVE INSTRUCTIONS:

Prepare leek as directed above. Combine leek, chicken broth and potato in a deep casserole with a lid. Add the curry powder and pepper. Microwave, covered, on **high** for 3 minutes. Reduce to **low** and continue to cook for about 10 minutes, or until leeks and potatoes are soft. Add peas; microwave on **high** 3 minutes more. Allow to cool slightly. Blend until smooth. Refrigerate. Stir in yogurt and skim milk just before serving.

Yield: 2 servings

1 Serving

Calories	97	Food Groups	
Protein	5 g	1 Bread	
Total Fat	0 g	1 Vegetable	
Saturated Fat	0 g		
Carbohydrate	19 g		
Cholesterol	1 mg		
Sodium	535 mg		

Serving Suggestion: Serve hot or cold. Increase quantity for a party and prepare a day ahead.

CHILLED CARROT AND CUCUMBER SOUP

¾ cup	diced, cooked carrots	175 mL
½ cup	diced cucumber	125 mL
1	garlic clove, minced	1
¼ tsp.	salt	1 mL
⅛ tsp.	white pepper	0.5 mL
⅔ cup	skim milk	150 mL
⅔ cup	low-fat yogurt	150 mL
1 tsp.	chopped chives or green onion	5 mL
	chopped parsley for garnish	

Chill carrots. Combine carrots, cucumber, garlic, salt, pepper and skim milk in blender. Blend until smooth. Stir in yogurt and chives. Pour into serving bowls and garnish with chopped parsley.

Yield: 2 servings

1 Serving

Calories	75	**Food Groups**	
Protein	6 g	1 Milk	
Total Fat	1 g	1 Vegetable	
Saturated Fat	0 g		
Carbohydrate	12 g		
Cholesterol	4 mg		
Sodium	339 mg		

Serving Suggestion: This is a flavorful change from a glass of milk. Serve with a sandwich on a hot day.

Meat, Fish & Poultry

SWEET AND SOUR MEATBALLS

8 oz.	lean ground beef	225 g
1	egg white	1
1 tbsp.	bread crumbs	15 mL
1	small onion, thinly sliced	1
1 tsp.	freshly grated ginger OR ½ tsp (2 mL) ground ginger	5 mL
1	garlic clove, minced	1
1 tbsp.	salt-reduced soy sauce	15 mL
½ tbsp.	vinegar	7 mL
1 tbsp.	brown sugar	15 mL
⅛ tsp.	red pepper flakes	0.5 mL
¾ cup	beef stock	175 mL
2 tsp.	cornstarch	10 mL
½ cup	coarsely chopped green pepper	125 mL
1	celery stalk, sliced	1
2	cherry tomatoes, quartered	2

Combine beef, egg white and bread crumbs. Mix well and shape into 12 small meatballs. Brown in a heavy frying pan sprayed with nonstick spray. Turn frequently and continue cooking until done, about 10 minutes. Remove meatballs and drain on paper towels. Drain fat from pan. Combine next 7 ingredients in same pan. Add ½ cup of the beef stock. Stir and cook about 5 minutes. Combine cornstarch with remaining ¼ cup (60 mL) of stock. Stir into sauce and cook, stirring constantly, until slightly thickened. Add meatballs and vegetables. Bring to a simmer and cook about 5 minutes. **Vegetables should not be soft.**

SWEET AND SOUR MEATBALLS (Cont'd.)

MICROWAVE INSTRUCTIONS:

Combine beef, egg white and bread crumbs. Mix well and shape into 12 small meatballs. Place in a pie plate, cover with waxed paper and microwave on **high** for 5 minutes, rotating at ½ time. Drain and set aside. In a microwave casserole, combine next 7 ingredients. Add ½ cup (125 mL) beef stock, cover and microwave on **high** for 5 to 7 minutes to soften onion. Combine cornstarch with remaining ¼ cup (60 mL) of stock, stir into sauce. Return to microwave on **high** for 1 minute to thicken. Add meatballs and vegetables. Microwave on **high** for 3 to 5 minutes to heat through and cook vegetables to tender-crisp stage.

Yield: 2 servings

1 Serving

		Food Groups
Calories	320	4 R Meat
Protein	28 g	½ Bread
Total Fat	14 g	1 Vegetable
Saturated Fat	6 g	1 tsp. Sugar
Carbohydrate	20 g	
Cholesterol	80 mg	
Sodium	778 mg	

Serving Suggestion: Serve over rice with added cooked vegetables on the side, if desired.

HAMBURGER STROGANOFF

8 oz.	lean ground beef	225 g
1	small onion, chopped	1
1	garlic clove, minced	1
⅛ tsp.	pepper	0.5 mL
¼ tsp.	paprika	1 mL
⅓ cup	condensed, low-calorie cream mushroom soup	75 mL
1 cup	sliced mushrooms	250 mL
¼ cup	2% yogurt	60 mL

Spray a frying pan with nonstick spray. Brown the ground beef and drain off any accumulated fat. Add onion, garlic, pepper, paprika and soup. Stir and cover. Simmer for 10 minutes, to cook onion and blend flavors. Stir in mushrooms and cook 5 minutes more. Stir in yogurt just before serving.

MICROWAVE INSTRUCTIONS:

Place the ground beef in a plastic colander over a pie plate or bowl. Microwave on **medium** for 3-4 minutes, stirring frequently, until all pink has disappeared. In a microwave casserole, place the meat, onion, garlic, pepper, paprika, and soup. Stir well and cover. Microwave on **medium** for 5 minutes. Stir halfway through. Add mushrooms and microwave on **medium** for 2 minutes more. Stir in yogurt just before serving.

Yield: 2 servings

1 Serving

Calories	292	Food Groups
Protein	28 g	4 R Meat
Total Fat	15 g	½ Bread
Saturated Fat	6 g	1 Vegetable
Carbohydrate	12 g	
Cholesterol	81 mg	
Sodium	468 mg	

Serving Suggestion: This is terrific on noodles. Add a colorful vegetable and salad.

BARLEY BURGER STEW

6 oz.	lean ground beef	180 g
½ cup	chopped onion	125 mL
½ cup	chopped celery	125 mL
½ cup	chopped green pepper	125 mL
1 cup	tomato or vegetable juice	250 mL
1 cup	beef broth or bouillon	250 mL
1 tsp.	chili powder	5 mL
¼ tsp	ground pepper	1 mL
¼ cup	pearl or pot barley	60 mL
1	small carrot, sliced	1

Spray a heavy saucepan with nonstick spray. Brown the ground beef and drain off any accumulated fat. Add the next 8 ingredients. Cover and simmer for 2 hours. Stir occasionally. Add sliced carrot; simmer for 15 minutes. Serve immediately.

MICROWAVE INSTRUCTIONS:

Place the beef in a plastic colander over a pie plate or bowl. Microwave on **medium** for 3-4 minutes, or until meat is no longer pink. Stir at half cooking time. Transfer the meat to a 3-quart (3 L) microwave container with a lid. Add the next 8 ingredients. Cover and microwave on **high** for 10 minutes. Reduce to **low** and continue for 45 minutes, stirring every 15 minutes. Check doneness of barley. When the barley is soft, add the sliced carrot and microwave on **medium** for 10 minutes, or until the carrots are tender but not soft. Do not overcook. Serve immediately.

Yield: 2 servings

1 Serving

		Food Groups
Calories	306	
Protein	23 g	3 R Meat
Total Fat	11 g	1 Bread
Saturated Fat	5 g	2 Vegetables
Carbohydrate	30 g	
Cholesterol	60 mg	
Sodium	712 mg	

Serving Suggestion: As this is a hefty serving, a green salad, and slice of fresh bread will satisfy most appetites.

CREOLE STUFFED PEPPERS

2	large green peppers	2
½ cup	water	125 mL
8 oz.	lean ground beef	225 g
¼ cup	diced celery	60 mL
½ cup	chopped onion	125 mL
1 cup	canned tomato sauce	250 mL
¼ tsp.	cinnamon	1 mL
3	whole cloves	3
⅛ tsp	cayenne pepper	0.5 mL

Cut the tops off the peppers. Throw away the stem but reserve the bit of pepper from the top and mince. Clean out the peppers and put them in ½ cup (125 mL) of water in a deep pot. Cover and cook for about 5 minutes to soften slightly. In a heavy skillet, sprayed with nonstick spray, brown the ground beef. Drain off any fat that accumulates. Mix the beef with the chopped green pepper, celery and half of the chopped onion. Fill the peppers with this mixture. Combine the tomato sauce, remaining onion and the seasonings. Cook for 5 minutes. Discard the cloves. Pour the sauce into a deep baking pan. Place the stuffed peppers in the sauce, spoon some sauce over peppers. Cover and bake in a 350°F (180°C) oven for 30 minutes, or until the peppers are tender.

CREOLE STUFFED PEPPERS
(Cont'd.)

MICROWAVE INSTRUCTIONS:

Cut the tops off the peppers, dice the bit of pepper from the top and throw away the stem. Clean out the peppers. In a deep casserole with a lid, place the peppers and ½ cup (125 mL) water. Cover and microwave on **high** for 5 minutes. Drain. In a plastic colander over a bowl or glass pie plate, brown the meat on **medium** for 4 minutes or until it is no longer pink. Stir after 2 minutes. Combine the meat with the chopped pepper, celery and half the onion. Stuff the peppers with the meat mixture. In a deep casserole combine the tomato sauce, remaining onion and seasonings. Cover and microwave on **high** for 3 minutes. Discard the cloves. Place the peppers in the sauce, spoon some sauce over peppers. Cover and microwave on **high** for 10 minutes, or until peppers are tender. Rotate and spoon more sauce over top after 5 minutes.

Yield: 2 servings

1 Serving		
Calories	263	**Food Groups**
Protein	24 g	3 R Meat
Fat	13 g	2 Vegetables
Saturated Fat	5 g	
Carbohydrate	12 g	
Cholesterol	60 mg	
Sodium	221 mg	

Serving Suggestion: This is a good meal to serve with rice, as there is sufficient sauce to use on the rice, as well as with the peppers.

TAMALE PIE

4 oz.	lean ground beef	120 g
¼ cup	chopped onion	60 mL
¼ cup	chopped celery	60 mL
¼ cup	chopped green pepper	60 mL
¼ cup	canned tomato sauce	60 mL
7 oz.	canned whole kernel corn	198 mL
¼ cup	sliced ripe olives	60 mL
1	garlic clove, minced	1
½ tsp.	chili powder	2 mL
⅛ tsp.	ground cumin	0.5 mL
2 oz.	low-fat cheese, grated	60 g

TOPPING:

¼ cup	cornmeal	60 mL
¾ cup	cold water	175 mL
⅛ tsp.	salt	0.5 mL
⅛ tsp	chili powder	0.5 mL

In a frying pan, sprayed with nonstick spray, brown the beef. Pour off any fat that accumulates. Add the onions, celery, green pepper and tomato sauce. Stir and cook for a few minutes, until vegetables are soft. Add remaining ingredients and stir well. Turn into a 4-cup (1 L) casserole, sprayed with nonstick spray. In a small saucepan, combine the cornmeal, cold water and salt. Bring to a boil, stirring constantly, until thickened. Stir in the chili powder. Spread topping over the tamale pie. Bake in a 350°F (180°C) oven for 15 minutes, or until topping has browned slightly and pie is bubbly. Makes 2 generous servings.

TAMALE PIE (Cont'd.)

MICROWAVE INSTRUCTIONS:

In a plastic colander over a bowl, brown the beef in the microwave on **medium** for 2 minutes. Stir and break up beef after 1 minute. In a microwave-safe casserole, combine the beef, onions, celery, green peppers and tomato sauce. Cover and microwave on **high** for 2 minutes to cook the vegetables. Add the remaining ingredients, stir well. In a glass measure, combine the cornmeal, water and salt. Microwave on **high** for 3 minutes stirring well after each minute has passed. Stir in the chili powder. Spread the topping over the tamale pie and microwave on **medium** for 3 minutes, or until topping has dried slightly and pie is bubbly.

Yield: 2 generous servings

1 serving

Calories	369	**Food Groups**
Protein	24 g	**3 R Meat**
Fat	14 g	**2 Bread**
Saturated Fat	5 g	**1 Vegetable**
Carbohydrate	40 g	
Cholesterol	82 mg	
Sodium	1403 mg	

FILET MIGNON WITH WINE MUSHROOM SAUCE

2 x 4 oz.	filet mignon	2 x 120g
¼ cup	strong beef bouillon	60 mL
¼ cup	red wine	60 mL
1 cup	sliced mushrooms	250 mL
⅛ tsp.	pepper	0.5 mL
1 tsp.	cornstarch	5 mL

If small filets are not available, consider buying a large 8 oz. (225 g) filet and slicing it in ½ crosswise, so it is less thick, but the right weight. If steaks are 2" (5 cm) thick, broil about 5 minutes for rare, 7 minutes for medium and 10 minutes for well done. Combine bouillon, wine, mushrooms and pepper in small saucepan. Simmer until mushrooms are cooked. Mix the cornstarch with 1 tsp. (5 mL) of water. Stir into sauce and stir until slightly thickened and clear. Serve over steaks.

MICROWAVE INSTRUCTIONS:

Broil steaks as usual. In a small casserole with a lid, combine bouillon, wine, mushrooms and pepper. Cover and microwave on **high** for 2 minutes, or until mushrooms are soft. Mix cornstarch with 1 tsp. (5 mL) of water and stir into sauce until it is slightly thickened and clear. Serve over steaks.

Yield: 2 servings

1 Serving

Calories	205	**Food Groups**	
Protein	26 g	3 L Meat	
Total Fat	7 g	1 Vegetable	
Saturated Fat	3 g		
Carbohydrate	6 g		
Cholesterol	58 mg		
Sodium	293 mg		

Serving suggestion: A baked potato, your favorite vegetable and salad and the bottle of red wine that was used for the sauce! What else?

See photograph opposite.

Filet Mignon With Wine Mushroom Sauce, page 80
Broiled Tomatoes, page 140
Savory Rice, page 142

GREEN PEPPER STEAK

8 oz.	inside round steak, cut into thin strips across the grain	225g
1 tbsp.	dry sherry	15 mL
2 tbsp.	salt-reduced soy sauce	30 mL
1 tbsp.	cooking oil	15 mL
1	medium onion, sliced thinly	1
1	medium green pepper, slivered	1
2 tsp.	cornstarch	10 mL
⅓ cup	water	75 mL

Combine steak, sherry and soy sauce in a bowl. If you have time, marinate for several hours. Otherwise, in a frying pan, heat the oil. Add the onion and cook briefly, move to one side and add the meat. Stir-fry until cooked through. Add the peppers and cook 1 minute. Mix the cornstarch with the water. Stir in all at once, stirring constantly until thickened and clear. Serve at once.

MICROWAVE INSTRUCTIONS:

Combine steak, sherry and soy sauce in a bowl. In a shallow casserole with a lid, combine the oil and onion. Cover and microwave on **high** 1 minute. Add the meat and sauce. Microwave on high 2 minutes, stirring every 30 seconds. Add the green pepper and microwave on **high** 1 minute more. Combine cornstarch and water, stir into meat and vegetables until thickened. Microwave on **high** 30 seconds more, if necessary. Serve at once.

Yield: 2 servings

1 Serving

		Food Groups
Calories	251	4 L Meat
Protein	28 g	1 Vegetable
Total Fat	11 g	
Saturated Fat	1 g	
Carbohydrate	9 g	
Cholesterol	55 mg	
Sodium	648 mg	

Serving Suggestions: Rice and another vegetable or salad will fill the bill.

FIERY LAMB BROIL

1 lb.	boneless lamb leg	454 g
1	garlic clove	1
¼ cup	minced onion	60 mL
1½ tbsp.	cooking oil	22 mL
2 tsp	tomato paste	10 mL
1½ tsp.	paprika	7 mL
¼ cup	red wine	60 mL

Cut the lamb into 8 pieces. Combine all of the other ingredients in a bowl. Add the lamb, stir well to coat evenly with the marinade. Cover and marinate for 24 hours before using. Lift the meat out of the marinade and place on a broiling pan that has been sprayed with a nonstick spray. Broil the meat, 4" (10 cm) from the heat, 4-5 minutes per side. Brush with the marinade frequently. Do not over cook or it will be dry.

Yield: 4 servings

1 Serving

Calories	243	Food Groups
Protein	29 g	4 L Meat
Total Fat	13 g	
Saturated Fat	5 g	
Carbohydrate	2 g	
Cholesterol	100 mg	
Sodium	71 mg	

Serving Suggestion: We are providing this recipe for 4 because it is a lovely dish for a small dinner party. Accompany with rice, rice and wild rice mix or couscous, brightly colored vegetables and a green salad.

PORK STROGANOFF

7 oz.	pork tenderloin	200 g
1	small onion, thinly sliced	1
½ tbsp.	flour	7 mL
½ cup	dry red wine	125 mL
½ tbsp.	tomato paste	7 mL
⅛ tsp.	salt	0.5 mL
⅛ tsp.	pepper	0.5 mL
2-3 drops	hot pepper sauce	2-3 drops
1 cup	sliced mushrooms	250 mL
2 tbsp.	low-fat yogurt	30 mL

Slice the tenderloin into thin medallions. In a frying pan, sprayed with nonstick spray, brown the meat. Add the onions and stir in the flour. Add wine and stir well to get up the brown bits. Add tomato paste, salt, pepper and hot pepper sauce. Simmer for 5 minutes. Add the mushrooms and simmer 5 minutes more. Stir in the yogurt and serve immediately.

MICROWAVE INSTRUCTIONS:

This dish is so quick to prepare that transferring it to the microwave after browning is a waste of time and dirties another dish!

Yield: 2 servings

1 Serving

Calories	216	Food Groups
Protein	28 g	4 L Meat
Total Fat	5 g	1 Vegetable
Saturated Fat	2 g	
Carbohydrate	9 g	
Cholesterol	84 mg	
Sodium	167 mg	

Serving Suggestion: Terrific with rice or noodles and a bright vegetable such as the Steamed Zucchini and Tomatoes, page 139.

SLIM MEAT PIE

1 lb.	lean ground pork	450 g
1 lb.	lean ground turkey	450 g
1 cup	finely chopped onion	250 mL
1	garlic clove, minced	1
½ tsp.	ground allspice	2 mL
½ tsp	ground cloves	2 mL
¼ tsp.	salt	1 mL
⅛ tsp.	pepper	0.5 mL
1 cup	water	250 mL
1	loaf frozen bread dough	1
1	egg, beaten	1
½ cup	mashed potato	125 mL
1 tbsp.	melted margarine	15 mL

Filling: Brown meat in a large skillet, breaking it up into small bits. Drain off any fat that accumulates. Add next 7 ingredients, bring to a boil and simmer, partially covered, for 30 minutes. Chill mixture while preparing dough.

MICROWAVE INSTRUCTIONS:

Filling: Place the meat in a microwave-safe colander over a pie plate or bowl. Microwave on **medium** 4-5 minutes, stirring frequently to break up, until all pink disappears. Transfer to a casserole with a lid. Add next 7 ingredients. Cover and microwave on **high** to bring to a boil. Reduce to **medium** for 10 minutes, or until cooked. Chill mixture while preparing dough.

SLIM MEAT PIE (Cont'd.)

See "quick thaw" method for dough, page 60.

Roll ⅔ of the thawed dough out to an 11" (30 cm) circle. Spray a 10" (25 cm) spring form pan with nonstick spray. Press dough into the bottom and up the sides about 1" (2.5 cm). Mix potato and egg and add to chilled meat mixture. Place in the dough "crust" and smooth out to the edges. Roll out the remaining dough to a 10" (25 cm) circle and cut into 8 wedges. Place these on top of the filling, overlapping slightly, if necessary, and sealing the outside edges. Brush with the melted margarine and bake at 375°F (190°C) for 30 minutes. Cool for 10 minutes on a rack. Remove pan sides and cut pie into 8 pieces. Serve warm.

Yield: 8 servings

1 serving

Calories	341	**Food Groups**
Protein	24 g	3 R Meat
Fat	13 g	2 Bread
Saturated Fat	5 g	
Carbohydrate	29 g	
Cholesterol	105 mg	
Sodium	612 mg	

Serving Suggestion: A colorful vegetable and salad are all that are needed to round out this meal. This is a low-fat version of a traditional French Canadian Christmas Eve "tourtiere" which is normally made with a regular pastry crust, which of course has a very high fat content.

PORK MEDALLIONS IN WHITE WINE

7 oz.	pork tenderloin	200 g
1	garlic clove, minced	1
½ tsp.	thyme	2 mL
¼ tsp.	salt	1 mL
⅛ tsp.	pepper	0.5 mL
½ cup	white wine	125 mL
½ cup	sliced mushrooms	125 mL
1	small tomato, peeled and diced	1

Slice pork tenderloin in ¼-½" (1 cm) thick medallions. Brown in frying pan sprayed with nonstick spray. Sprinkle with garlic, thyme, salt and pepper. Pour white wine over and stir to pick up any browned bits on bottom of pan. Cover and cook 5 minutes. Add mushrooms and tomato. Cook, uncovered, 5 minutes more. Spoon the sauce over the meat to serve.

MICROWAVE INSTRUCTIONS:

This dish is so quick to prepare that there is no advantage to using the microwave here. It only dirties another dish!

Yield: 2 servings

1 Serving

		Food Groups
Calories	164	
Protein	27 g	4 L Meat
Total Fat	5 g	1 Vegetable
Saturated Fat	2 g	
Carbohydrate	3 g	
Cholesterol	84 mg	
Sodium	302 mg	

Serving Suggestion: Red or green pasta, a vegetable and salad complete this meal.

ITALIAN PORK CHOP BAKE

2	loin pork chops, trim fat	2
¼ tsp.	crushed oregano leaves	1 mL
¼ tsp.	crushed basil leaves	1 mL
¼ tsp.	garlic powder	1 mL
⅛ tsp.	black pepper	0.5 mL
1	large onion, sliced	1
⅔ cup	raw macaroni	150 mL
14 oz.	canned tomatoes and juice	398 mL
¼ cup	chopped green pepper	60 mL
¼ cup	chopped celery	60 mL

In heavy frying pan, sprayed with nonstick spray, brown the chops over medium heat. As they are browning, sprinkle them with oregano, basil, garlic and pepper. After they are browned, reduce heat and cover them with the sliced onion and macaroni. Break up the tomatoes and combine with the green pepper and celery. Pour tomato mixture over the macaroni. Stir, making sure all of the macaroni is covered by the liquid. Cover and simmer for 30 minutes, or until done.

MICROWAVE INSTRUCTIONS:

Brown chops, as above. Sprinkle with oregano, basil, garlic and pepper. Place chops in a microwave-safe casserole with a lid. Cover with sliced onion, and macaroni. Place the tomatoes, pepper and celery in the frying pan. Break up the tomatoes and stir to pick up any herbs and browned bit of chops. Pour tomato mixture over the macaroni. Cover and microwave on **medium** for 20 minutes total. Rotate and stir gently after 10 minutes.

Yield: 2 servings

1 Serving

Calories	418	**Food Groups**
Protein	29 g	4 R Meat
Fat	14 g	2 Bread
Saturated Fat	6 g	2 Vegetables
Carbohydrate	44 g	
Cholesterol	82 mg	
Sodium	376 mg	

Serving Suggestion: This is almost a meal in itself, but you may want a second vegetable or a salad to accompany it.

CARIBBEAN PORK ROAST

1 lb.	boneless pork loin roast	450-500 g
⅛ tsp.	black pepper	0.5 mL
⅛ tsp.	salt	0.5 mL
½ tsp.	ground ginger	2 mL
⅛ tsp.	ground nutmeg	0.5 mL
⅛ tsp.	ground cloves	0.5 mL
⅛ tsp.	ground cinnamon	0.5 mL
⅛ tsp.	garlic powder	0.5 mL
2 tsp.	brown sugar	10 mL
1	small bay leaf, crumbled	1
2 tbsp.	lemon juice	30 mL
¼ cup	chicken broth	60 mL
¼ cup	orange juice	60 mL
¼ cup	rum	60 mL
1 tsp.	cornstarch	5 mL
1 tbsp.	water	15 mL

Lay roast in a roasting pan. Combine the pepper, salt, ginger, nutmeg, cloves, cinnamon, and garlic powder. Pat onto the roast until it is covered. Pat on the brown sugar and lay the crumbled bay leaf on top. Combine the lemon juice, chicken broth, orange juice and rum and pour around roast, not on top of it. Roast, covered, in a 350°F (180°C) oven for 45 minutes, or until meat is cooked. Allow juices to boil down and brown a bit. Remove the roast to a serving platter. Mix the cornstarch with cold water. Defat the roast juices and heat on top of the stove. Stir in the cornstarch, cook and stir just until smooth and clear. Serve, in a separate container, with the roast.

MICROWAVE INSTRUCTIONS:

Prepare roast as above. Place in a microwave roaster with lid. Microwave on **low** 11-13 minutes. Test for doneness. Remove the roast and defat the juices. Place juices in a glass measure. Microwave on **high** 1 minute. Meanwhile, mix the cornstarch with cold water. Stir cornstarch into hot juices and stir until clear and slightly thickened. Return to microwave for a few seconds, if necessary, and stir again. Serve, in a separate container, with the roast.

Yield: 4 servings

CARIBBEAN PORK ROAST
(Cont'd.)

1 serving

Calories	176	Food Groups
Protein	26 g	4 L Meat
Total Fat	4 g	
Saturated Fat	2 g	
Carbohydrate	3 g	
Cholesterol	84 mg	
Sodium	178 mg	

Serving Suggestion: The sauce is excellent for both the meat and whatever starch you serve. We used cooked couscous and it was terrific! Marvelous reheated, too.

MICROWAVING FISH

Microwaving produces moist and flavorful seafood dishes. Because fish cooks very quickly and over-cooking tends to dry and toughen it, check after minimum time for doneness. Cook only until the outer areas are opaque and the center is slightly translucent. It will continue to cook during the standing stage.

TO DEFROST:

Place unopened packages in the microwave and defrost until the outer pieces start to loosen, but do not feel warm. Hold pieces of fish under running water until they can be separated.

TO COOK:

Cook fish on **high** power. Arrange fish in single layer with the thickest parts to the outside of the dish. Cover fish with waxed paper to hold in heat except when poaching, then it should be covered tightly. Use white wine or water with lemon juice as the poaching liquid.

MICROWAVE HINT

Remember some foods continue to cook after they are removed from the microwave oven.

WINE-POACHED TROUT

10 oz.	cleaned trout*	300 g
½ tsp.	salt	2 mL
⅛ tsp.	white pepper	0.5 mL
3-4	lemon slices	3-4
¼ cup	sliced green onion	60 mL
1 tsp.	chopped parsley	5 mL
½ cup	white wine	125 mL
½ cup	water	125 mL
¼ cup	lemon juice	60 mL
	lemon wedges and parsley	

* a 1 lb. (500 g) fish yields about 10 oz. (300 g) cleaned.

Wash trout. Sprinkle inside and out with salt and pepper. Stuff lemon slices, onion and parsley in the body cavity. Lay fish in a frying pan. Add wine, water and lemon juice. Cover and bring to a boil. Reduce to a simmer for approximately 6-7 minutes, or until flesh flakes easily. Remove the fish. Simmer sauce until reduced to about ½ cup (125 mL). Skin the fish. Run a sharp knife along the top of the bones. Carefully lift off the fillet with a spatula. Lift bones out of the second fillet. Place fillets on a serving platter, pour the sauce over. Garnish with lemon wedges and fresh parsley.

MICROWAVE INSTRUCTIONS:

Prepare exactly as above. Use a microwave baking pan, cover and microwave on **high** 4-5 minutes, or until fish flakes. Turn the pan around at ½ time. Remove fish, return juices to the oven; microwave, uncovered, on **high** 3-4 minutes, or until reduced to ½ cup (125 mL). Serve as above.

Yield 2 servings

1 Serving

Calories	182	Food Groups
Protein	22 g	3 L Meat
Total Fat	6 g	
Saturated Fat	1 g	
Cholesterol	51 mg	
Sodium	600 mg	

Serving Suggestion: A baked potato plus a colorful vegetable and salad will complement this dish nicely.

SOLE WITH SPINACH & CRAB

7 oz.	sole fillets	200 g
1 tbsp.	lemon juice	15 mL
1 cup	drained cooked spinach	250 mL
1 oz.	chopped crab or mock crab	30 g
½ cup	skim milk	125 mL
1 tbsp.	flour	15 mL
¼ cup	skim milk	60 mL
½ tsp.	prepared mustard	2 mL
½ tsp.	Worcestershire sauce	2 mL
⅛ tsp.	white pepper	0.5 mL
	paprika (optional)	

Lay fillets in a baking dish. Sprinkle with lemon juice. Combine spinach with chopped crab. Spread over the fillets. Heat the first amount of milk in a small saucepan. Blend flour with second amount of milk until smooth. Whisk into heated milk until thickened. Add mustard, Worcestershire and pepper. Pour over fish. Sprinkle with paprika, if desired. Bake at 350°F (180°C) for 20-30 minutes.

MICROWAVE INSTRUCTIONS:

Lay fillets in microwave baking dish. Sprinkle with lemon juice. Combine spinach and crab and spread over fillets. In a glass measure, microwave the first amount of milk on **high** for 1 minute, or until it begins to boil. Blend the flour with the second amount of milk until smooth. Whisk into heated milk until thickened. Add the mustard, Worcestershire and pepper. Pour over fish and spinach. Sprinkle with paprika, if desired. Cover and microwave on **high** 4 minutes, then on **medium** 6-8 minutes, until fish is opaque and flakes easily.

Yield: 2 servings

1 Serving

		Food Groups
Calories	265	
Protein	35 g	4 L Meat
Total Fat	8 g	1 Vegetable
Saturated Fat	2 g	1 Milk
Carbohydrate	12 g	
Cholesterol	93 mg	
Sodium	364 mg	

Serving Suggestion: Fish is soft in texture, so try to have a firm vegetable with it, plus a starch, such as a baked potato.

CRISP SESAME FILLETS

1 tbsp.	cooking oil	15 mL
7 oz.	fish fillets, 1 large or 2 small	200 g
2 tbsp.	low-fat yogurt	30 mL
2 tbsp.	bread crumbs	30 mL
1 tbsp.	sesame seeds	15 mL
½ tsp.	dillweed	2 mL
	lemon wedges	

Spray a heavy frying pan with nonstick spray. Heat on medium and add ½ of the cooking oil. Pat the fillets dry and coat, one at a time, with the yogurt. Combine bread crumbs, sesame seeds and dillweed in a flat dish. Roll the fillets in the bread-crumb mixture, coat well and place in the hot frying pan. Repeat with second fillet. If fillets are thin, they will only take 2-3 minutes per side to cook. Add remaining oil when fillets are being turned over, so they do not stick. Remove fillets to hot platter and serve with lemon wedges.

Yield: 2 servings

1 Serving

Calories	283	**Food Groups**	
Protein	29 g	4 L Meat	
Total Fat	15 g*	1 Fat	
Saturated Fat	2 g	½ Bread	
Carbohydrate	7 g		
Cholesterol	82 mg	267 mg	
	Sodium		

Serving Suggestion: Terrific with Homemade Low-Fat Home Fries, page 148 and a bright vegetable such as broccoli, carrots or hot pickled beets, page 147.

* This figure is based on all of the fat being absorbed by the fish as it cooks. If this is not the case, the fat content would be lower.

WINE & MUSHROOM FILLETS

1 tsp.	margarine	5 mL
4	large mushrooms, sliced	4
8 oz.	fish fillets, fresh or frozen	225 g
1/4 cup	white wine	60 mL
1 tbsp.	lime juice	15 mL
1 tsp.	dried parsley	5 mL
1/8 tsp.	garlic powder	0.5 mL
1/4 tsp.	dry mustard	1 mL
1/4 tsp.	dillweed	1 mL
1/8 tsp.	white pepper	0.5 mL

In a medium-sized frying pan with a lid, melt margarine and add mushrooms. Simmer for about 2 minutes, until mushrooms are soft. Remove mushrooms. Lay the fish fillets in the frying pan, cover them with the mushrooms. Combine remaining ingredients, stir and pour over the fish. Cover and simmer for 3 minutes. Remove cover and simmer for another 3 to 4 minutes, to reduce the sauce and thicken it slightly.

MICROWAVE INSTRUCTIONS:

Place margarine and mushrooms in a shallow dish with a lid. Microwave on **high** for 1 minute. Lay fish fillets in a shallow casserole, cover with mushrooms. Combine remaining ingredients, stir and pour over fish and mushrooms. Cover and microwave on **medium** for 5 minutes, or until fish flakes. Rotate at half time. Remove fish to serving platter. Microwave sauce 1-2 minutes, uncovered, to reduce and thicken slightly.

Yield: 2 servings

1 Serving

Calories	241	Food Groups	
Protein	32 g	4 L Meat	
Fat	11 g		
Saturated Fat	2 g		
Carbohydrate	3 g		
Cholesterol	93 mg		
Sodium	272 mg		

Serving Suggestion: This sauce is quite lovely, cook a bit of fresh tomato or spinach pasta to go with this, plus a vegetable and a salad.

FILLETS & CHEESE SAUCE

8 oz.	white fish fillets	225 g
½ cup	skim milk	125 mL
2 tbsp.	skim milk	30 mL
2 tbsp.	flour	30 mL
½ tsp.	Worcestershire sauce	2 mL
⅛ tsp.	white pepper	0.5 mL
1 oz.	old Cheddar cheese, grated	30 g
2 tbsp.	white wine	30 mL
	paprika	

Spray (a glass loaf pan) with nonstick spray. Arrange the fillets in 1 layer. Heat first amount of milk in the top of a double boiler. Mix second amount of milk with flour and stir to dissolve. Add Worcestershire and pepper. Add the flour mixture to the hot milk, beating constantly until thickened. Add grated cheese and stir until melted. Stir in wine and pour sauce over fillets. Sprinkle with paprika. Bake at 350°F (180°C) for 20 minutes, until fillets are opaque and flake easily.

MICROWAVE INSTRUCTIONS:

Lay fillets in 1 layer in a small casserole sprayed with nonstick spray. In a glass measure, place the first amount of milk. Microwave on **high** for 1 minute. Combine second amount of milk with flour; stir to dissolve. Add Worcestershire and pepper. Whisk into hot milk. Microwave on **high** for 30 seconds, whisk again. If not thickened, repeat. Stir in cheese. Add wine; stir and pour sauce over fillets. Sprinkle with paprika. Microwave on **medium** for 6-8 minutes, rotate after 4 minutes. Fish should be opaque and flake easily.

Yield: 2 servings

1 Serving

Calories	296	Food Groups	
Protein	34 g	4 L Meat	
Total Fat	12 g	1 Skim Milk	
Saturated Fat	5 g		
Carbohydrate	10 g		
Cholesterol	97 mg		
Sodium	347 mg		

Serving Suggestion: Baked Potatoes are great with this sauce.

STIR-FRIED FISH AND VEGETABLES

¼ cup	white wine	60 mL
1 tbsp.	salt-reduced soy sauce	15 mL
1	garlic clove, minced	1
¼ tsp.	vegetable seasoning*	1 mL
½ tbsp.	cornstarch	7 mL
1 tbsp.	cooking oil	15 mL
7 oz.	firm-fleshed fish, red snapper, swordfish, orange roughy	200 g
1	green onion, sliced	1
1 cup	broccoli florets**	250 mL
½ cup	green peas	125 mL
½ cup	sliced celery	125 mL
	water as required	
2	cherry tomatoes, halved	2
1 tsp.	slivered almonds	5 mL

* Dehydrated vegetable flakes to replace salt

**Any green vegetable may be used instead of broccoli.

Combine the wine, soy sauce, garlic, vegetable seasoning and cornstarch. Set aside. Heat oil in wok or frying pan. Cut the fish into bite-sized chunks and stir-fry for 2-3 minutes. Remove from pan. Add the onion, broccoli, peas and celery and a bit of water. Cover and cook until still slightly crisp. Add sauce and stir until thickened. Add more water, if necessary. Add fish and reheat. Garnish with cherry tomatoes and almonds.

Yield: 2 servings

1 Serving

Calories	338	**Food Groups**
Protein	32 g	4 L Meat
Total Fat	16 g	2 Vegetables
Saturated Fat	2 g	
Carbohydrate	15 g	
Cholesterol	81 mg	
Sodium	569 mg	

Serving Suggestion: Rice is all you need to complete this filling dish.

SALMON STEAKS WITH DILL SAUCE

2 x 4 oz.	salmon steaks	2 x 120 g
2 tbsp.	calorie-reduced mayonnaise	30 mL
3 tbsp.	lemon juice	45 mL
¼ tsp.	dried dillweed	1 mL
⅛ tsp.	white pepper	0.5 mL

Spray broiling pan with nonstick spray. Place steaks on broiling pan. Combine remaining ingredients to make sauce. Broil salmon steaks 3 minutes, 5" (12 cm) from heat. Turn the steaks over and spread the sauce evenly over them. Broil for 3 minutes more. Follow the same instructions for your barbecue. Serve immediately.

MICROWAVE INSTRUCTIONS:

Place steaks on a baking rack with ridges, to allow fat to drip away, in a shallow pan. Cover with waxed paper. Microwave on high for 2 minutes. Combine remaining ingredients to make sauce. Spread steaks with sauce; cover loosely with waxed paper. Microwave on **high** 2 minutes more. Serve immediately.

Yield: 2 servings

1 Serving

Calories	203	Food Groups
Protein	23 g	3 R Meat
Total Fat	10 g	
Saturated Fat	2 g	
Carbohydrate	4 g	
Cholesterol	40 mg	
Sodium	102 mg	

Serving Suggestion: All this needs is a beautiful baked potato and a vegetable to make a marvelous meal, in no time at all! A terrific way to start the barbecue season!

Shrimp With Snow Peas, page 99

SALMON LOAF

7.5 oz.	can pink or red salmon	213 g
1	egg	1
½ cup	mashed potato	125 mL
1 tbsp.	lemon juice	15 mL
2 tsp.	grated onion*	10 mL
1 tsp.	grated horseradish	5 mL
½ tsp.	paprika	2 mL
¼ tsp.	dry mustard	1 mL
¼ tsp.	dillweed	1 mL

*Peel a small onion. Using the fine side of your grater, grate over waxed paper the amount of onion you need. Wrap the onion and refrigerate.

Spray a 2-cup (500 mL) casserole with nonstick spray. Drain salmon and place in a medium bowl. Using a fork, break up the salmon and add all of the remaining ingredients. Press mixture lightly into the casserole. Bake at 350°F (180°C) for 45 minutes.

MICROWAVE INSTRUCTIONS:

Prepare recipe as above. Microwave at **medium** 10 minutes, rotating at half time.

Yield: 2 servings

1 Serving

Calories	267	Food Groups
Protein	23 g	3 R Meat
Total Fat	15 g	½ Bread
Saturated Fat	5 g	
Carbohydrate	8 g	
Cholesterol	36 mg	
Sodium	418 mg	

Note: While the total fat content is relatively high, notice that the saturated fat is only ⅓ of the total fat, thus in keeping with healthy eating guidelines.

CURRIED TUNA

½ tbsp.	cooking oil	7 mL
1	small onion, chopped	1
1	garlic clove, minced	1
1	celery stalk, sliced	1
2 tsp.	flour	10 mL
1¼ tsp.	curry powder	6 mL
⅛ tsp.	white pepper	0.5 mL
½ cup	chicken stock or bouillon	125 mL
2 tbsp.	raisins	30 mL
6½ oz.	can solid chunk tuna	184 g
⅓ cup	chopped fresh apple, skin on	75 mL

In a heavy saucepan, heat the oil slightly. Add the onion, garlic and celery. Cook until softened. Stir in the flour, curry powder and pepper. Add the chicken stock, and stir to avoid lumps, while thickening slightly. Mix in the raisins and tuna and cook for 3 minutes. Stir in the apple and cook for 1 minute more.

MICROWAVE INSTRUCTIONS:

In a casserole, place the oil, onion, garlic and celery. Stir. Cover and microwave on **high** for 3 minutes. Stir in the flour and seasonings. Add the chicken stock and stir, to avoid lumps, while thickening slightly. Microwave on **high** for 30 seconds. Stir again. Add the raisins and tuna and microwave on medium for 2 minutes. Stir in the apple and microwave on medium 30 seconds more.

Yield: 2 servings

1 Serving

Calories	281	Food Groups
Protein	25 g	3 R Meat
Total Fat	11 g	1 Fruit
Saturated Fat	1 g	1 Vegetable
Carbohydrate	21 g	
Cholesterol	53 mg	
Sodium	887 mg	

Serving Suggestion: Rice, a bright vegetable and a salad make this a complete dinner.

SHRIMP WITH SNOW PEAS

2 tsp.	cooking oil	10 mL
1 cup	snow peas	250 mL
2	green onions, sliced	2
4-5	small mushrooms, sliced	4-5
6 oz.	cooked or cleaned raw shrimp	180 g
2 tsp.	soy sauce	10 mL
1	garlic clove, minced	1
½ tsp.	cornstarch	2 mL
⅓ cup	chicken broth	75 mL

In a frying pan or wok, heat the oil. Add the snow peas, onions and mushrooms. Cook for 2 minutes. Add the shrimp, soy sauce and garlic and continue to stir-fry for 3 minutes more. Mix the cornstarch with the chicken broth. Add all at once to the frying pan, stirring constantly until slightly thickened. Serve immediately.

Yield: 2 servings

1 Serving

Calories	224	**Food Groups**	
Protein	26 g	3 L Meat	
Total Fat	7 g	2 Vegetables	
Saturated Fat	0		
Carbohydrate	16 g		
Cholesterol	128 mg		
Sodium	801 mg		

Serving Suggestion: All stir-fries are great with rice. We hasten to add that many vegetables are suitable for stir-frying so, if snow peas aren't available, use any others you enjoy.

See photograph page 96A.

MALAY SHRIMP CURRY

2 tsp.	soft margarine	10 mL
½ cup	minced onion	125 mL
¼	English cucumber, sliced	¼
1	garlic clove, minced	1
2 tsp.	curry powder	10 mL
⅛ tsp.	cardamom	0.5 mL
1 tsp.	lemon juice	5 mL
¼ tsp.	ginger	1 mL
½ cup	skim milk	125 mL
1 tsp.	flour	5 mL
1	small tomato, peeled & diced	1
6 oz.	peeled shrimp	180 g

Melt margarine in frying pan. Add onion, cucumber, garlic, curry powder, cardamom, lemon juice and ginger. Simmer for 10 minutes. Mix the skim milk with the flour and quickly stir into the vegetables. Add the tomato and shrimp, cover and cook just until all shrimp are pink, about 5 minutes.

MICROWAVE INSTRUCITONS:

Melt margarine in a microwave casserole on **high** for 15 seconds. Add the onion, cucumber, garlic, curry powder, cardamom, lemon juice and ginger. Cover and microwave on **medium** for 5-6 minutes, until onion is soft. Mix the milk and flour and whisk into the vegetables. Microwave on **high** 30 seconds, to thicken. Add shrimp and tomato. Microwave on **medium** 2-3 minutes, until all shrimp are pink.

Yield: 2 servings

1 serving		
Calories	206	**Food Groups**
Protein	25 g	3 L Meat
Total Fat	6 g	1 Vegetable
Saturated Fat	2 g	½ Milk
Carbohydrate	14 g	
Cholesterol	129 mg	
Sodium	201 mg	

Note: Adjust curry powder and ginger for milder or hotter.

CHICKEN PAPRIKA

2	½ chicken breasts, boned, skin removed	2
½ tsp.	paprika	2 mL
½ cup	chicken bouillon	125 mL
½ cup	minced onion	125 mL
2 tsp.	paprika	10 mL
¼ cup	skim milk	60 mL
2 tsp.	flour	10 mL
2 tbsp.	medium-fat (3-4%MF) yogurt	30 mL

Spray a heavy frying pan with nonstick spray. Sprinkle the chicken with the first amount of paprika and brown in the frying pan. Add the chicken bouillon, onion and second amount of paprika. Stir well to pick up all the browned bits. Simmer, covered, for 15 minutes. Remove chicken pieces to a serving platter. Mix the skim milk and flour until smooth. Whisk into the chicken liquid until thickened. Stir in the yogurt just before serving and heat through. Pour sauce over chicken.

MICROWAVE INSTRUCTIONS:

Brown chicken as above. Remove chicken to a microwave casserole with a lid. Add bouillon, onion and second amount of paprika to frying pan, scrape up all the browned bits and pour over chicken. Cover and microwave on **high** for 7-10 minutes, or until chicken is cooked. Remove chicken pieces to a serving platter. Mix the skim milk and flour until smooth. Whisk into chicken liquid; microwave on **high** for 1 minute, stir well. Before serving, stir in yogurt, microwave on **high** for 30 seconds to heat. Pour over chicken.

Yield: 2 servings

1 Serving

Calories	148	Food Groups
Protein	23 g	3 L Meat
Total Fat	2 g	1 Vegetable
Saturated Fat	1 g	
Carbohydrate	8 g	
Cholesterol	54 mg	
Sodium	318 mg	

Serving Suggestion: Serve with cooked noodles or spatzle, page 117.

CHICKEN CREOLE

2	½ chicken breasts, boned, skin removed	2
½ cup	minced onion	125 mL
¼ cup	minced green pepper	60 mL
¼ cup	minced celery	60 mL
1 cup	canned tomatoes	250 mL
1	garlic clove, minced	1
½ tsp	crushed basil leaves	2 mL
⅛ tsp	cayenne pepper	0.5 mL
¼ cup	sliced ripe olives	60 mL
3	medium mushrooms, sliced	3

Brown the chicken breasts in a frying pan sprayed with non-stick spray. In a saucepan, combine the onions, green pepper, celery and juice from the tomatoes. Bring to a boil and simmer 5 minutes, to soften vegetables. Crush tomatoes, add garlic, basil, cayenne and cooked vegetables. Pour over chicken. Cover and simmer for 15 minutes, or until the chicken is cooked. Stir in olives and mushrooms; cook 5 minutes.

MICROWAVE INSTRUCTIONS:

Brown chicken breasts as above. In a glass measure, combine the onions, green pepper, celery and the juice from the tomatoes. Cover and microwave on **high** for 4 minutes, to soften the vegetables. Crush tomatoes, add garlic, basil, cayenne and vegetables. Pour sauce over chicken in a small microwave casserole and cover. Microwave on **medium** for 6-8 minutes. Stir in olives and mushrooms; microwave on **high** 3 minutes.

Yield: 2 servings

1 Servings

Calories	234	Food Groups
Protein	31 g	4 L Meat
Total Fat	8 g	1 Vegetable
Saturated Fat	2 g	
Carbohydrate	10 g	
Cholesterol	77 mg	
Sodium	1002 mg	

Serving Suggestion: Serve with rice, a green vegetable and/or salad.

CHICKEN GUMBO

2	chicken legs, skin removed*	2
1	small onion, chopped	1
1 cup	sliced okra	250 mL
14 oz.	can tomatoes	398 mL
¼ cup	raw rice	60 mL
1	garlic clove, minced	1
⅛ tsp.	thyme	0.5 mL
⅛ tsp.	cayenne pepper	0.5 mL
½ cup	water	125 mL
½ cup	whole kernel corn	125 mL

*Breast meat may be used, but this is a nice way to use chicken legs. Separate the thigh and lower leg to make 4 pieces.

Brown chicken in a frying pan sprayed with nonstick spray. Combine all other ingredients, except corn. Stir well. When chicken is browned, place in a deep casserole with a lid. Pour the tomato mixture over. Cover and bake at 350°F (180°C) for 30 to 40 minutes. Stir in corn and bake 10 minutes more.

MICROWAVE INSTRUCTIONS:

Brown chicken as above. Combine all other ingredients, except corn. Stir well. When chicken is browned, place in a microwave casserole with a lid. Pour tomato mixture over and cover. Microwave on **medium** for 30 minutes. Stir each 10 minutes and stir in the corn after 25 minutes.

Yield: 2 generous servings

1 Serving

Calories	338	Food Groups	
Protein	24 g	3 L Meat	
Fat	8 g	2 Bread	
Saturated Fat	2 g	2 Vegetables	
Carbohydrate	44 g		
Cholesterol	52 mg		
Sodium	707 mg		

Serving Suggestion: Accompany with a green vegetable and a salad. Leftover corn can be added to vegetable soup.

MEDITERRANEAN CHICKEN

1	medium eggplant	1
	salt	
2	½ chicken breasts, skinned	2
½ cup	chopped onion	125 mL
1	garlic clove, minced	1
½ cup	tomato sauce	125 mL
¼ tsp.	crushed oregano leaves	1 mL
¼ tsp.	Worcestershire sauce	1 mL
¼ tsp.	paprika	1 mL
⅛ tsp.	ground black pepper	0.5 mL

Peel and slice eggplant. Place in a colander and sprinkle with salt, to remove excess liquid from the eggplant. Brown chicken breasts in a frying pan sprayed with nonstick spray. Add remaining ingredients. Rinse salt off eggplant and add eggplant slices to the chicken and sauce. Simmer for 15-20 minutes, or until chicken is well done.

MICROWAVE INSRUCTIONS:

Peel and slice eggplant. Place in a colander and sprinkle with salt. Brown chicken breasts in a frying pan sprayed with nonstick spray. Transfer to a medium casserole with a lid. Add remaining ingredients and stir gently to mix. Rinse salt off eggplant and add it to the chicken and sauce. Cover and microwave on **medium** for 10 minutes, rotating and gently stirring at ½ time. Check chicken for doneness. Microwave a few minutes more, if necessary.

Yield: 2 servings

1 serving

Calories	235	Food Groups
Protein	29 g	4 L Meat
Total Fat	3 g	3 Vegetables
Saturated Fat	1 g	
Carbohydrate	25 g	
Cholesterol	65 mg	
Sodium	152 mg	

Serving Suggestion: Rice or your favorite pasta goes well with this interesting dish.

LEMON CHICKEN

2 tsp.	honey	10 mL
1 tbsp.	lemon juice	15 mL
1 tsp.	dried parsley flakes OR 1 tbsp. (15 mL) fresh chopped parsley	5 mL
¼ tsp.	salt	1 mL
⅛ tsp.	white pepper	0.5 mL
2	½ chicken breasts, boned, skin removed	2

Spray a broiling pan or metal pie pan with nonstick spray. Heat the honey, in a small container over hot water, to completely liquify. Add remaining ingredients, except chicken, to the honey. Spoon sauce over the chicken and broil 5" (13 cm) from heat. Turn, baste and continue to broil until chicken is done, 10 to 15 minutes.

MICROWAVE INSTRUCTIONS:

Brown chicken in a frying pan sprayed with nonstick spray. Transfer chicken to a microwave-safe casserole with a lid. Heat honey in the microwave for 15 seconds on **medium** to liquify. Combine honey with remaining ingredients. Spoon over the chicken pieces; cover and microwave on **medium** for 7-10 minutes, rotating the pan and basting every 3-4 minutes with the lemon honey mixture.

Yield: 2 servings

1 Serving

Calories	117	Food Groups
Protein	21 g	3 L Meat
Total Fat	1 g	
Saturated Fat	0	
Carbohydrate	5 g	
Cholesterol	52 mg	
Sodium	300 mg	

Serving Suggestion: Lovely with rice and brightly colored vegetables. This is a very light meal.

CHICKEN IN ORANGE GINGER SAUCE

2	½ chicken breasts boned, skin removed	2
1 tbsp.	flour	15 mL
½ cup	water	125 mL
1 tsp.	brown sugar	5 mL
1-2 drops	hot pepper sauce	1-2 drops
¼ tsp.	ground ginger	1 mL
⅛ tsp	salt	0.5 mL
½ tsp.	paprika	2 mL
⅓ cup	orange juice	75 mL
½	orange thinly sliced	½

In a heavy frying pan, sprayed, with nonstick spray, brown the chicken parts. Dissolve the flour in the water, add all of the other seasonings and orange juice. Pour over the chicken; stir to pick up any browned bits and to thicken the sauce slightly. Cover; simmer for 10 minutes, until chicken is cooked. Add the orange slices, heat for a minute and serve.

MICROWAVE INSTRUCTIONS:

In a heavy frying pan, sprayed with nonstick spray, brown the chicken parts. Transfer chicken to a microwave dish with a lid. Dissolve the flour in the water, add all of the other seasonings and orange juice. Pour into the frying pan. Simmer and stir to thicken slightly and pick up browned bits of chicken. Pour sauce over the chicken, cover and microwave on **medium** 5-7 minutes or until chicken is cooked. Add orange slices, microwave on **medium** 30 seconds more and serve.

Yield: 2 servings

1 Serving

Calories	191	Food Groups
Protein	27 g	4 L Meat
Total Fat	3 g	1 Fruit
Saturated Fat	1 g	
Carbohydrate	13 g	
Cholesterol	69 mg	
Sodium	153 mg	

CHICKEN HAWAIIAN

2	chicken legs OR 2, ½ chicken breasts, skinned	2
½ cup	unsweetened pineapple juice from tidbits below	125 mL
1 tbsp.	soy sauce	15 mL
1 tbsp.	brown sugar	15 mL
1 tbsp.	vinegar	15 mL
1 tbsp.	minced onion	15 mL
½ cup	pineapple tidbits	125 mL
½ cup	sliced fresh mushrooms	125 mL
⅛ tsp.	white pepper	0.5 mL
1 tsp.	cornstarch	5 mL
1 tsp.	water	5 mL

In a small heavy frying pan, sprayed with nonstick spray, brown the chicken pieces. Combine the pineapple juice, soy sauce, brown sugar, vinegar and onion, and pour over chicken. Cover and simmer for 20 minutes, or until chicken is almost cooked. Add the pineapple, mushrooms and white pepper. Stir, cover and simmer for 5 minutes. Dissolve cornstarch in water. Add to sauce, stirring until thickened and clear. Serve at once.

MICROWAVE INSTRUCTIONS:

Brown chicken as above. Transfer to a small casserole with cover. Pour pineapple juice, soy sauce, brown sugar, vinegar and onion into frying pan; stir well. Pour over the chicken, cover and microwave on **medium** 10 minutes, turning after 5 minutes. Add the pineapple, mushrooms and white pepper. Stir; microwave on **medium** 5 minutes. Dissolve cornstarch in water. Add to the sauce, stirring until thickened and clear. Return to microwave for 1 minute, if necessary.

Yield: 2 servings

1 Serving

		Food Groups
Calories	300	
Protein	28 g	4 L Meat
Total Fat	8 g	1 Fruit
Saturated Fat	2 g	1 Vegetable
Carbohydrate	30 g	2 tsp. sugar
Cholesterol	89 mg	
Sodium	597 mg	

ROAST CORNISH GAME HENS

1 to 1½ lb.	game hen	450-700 g
1 tsp.	melted margarine or butter	5 mL
	stuffing, pages 120-122	

Rinse the hen and pat dry. Stuff with one of the stuffings suggested or your own. Brush with melted margarine. Roast, uncovered, at 400°F (200°C) for 20 minutes. Turn and baste. Roast 20 minutes longer, baste again and turn so that the whole bird will be nicely browned. Roast another 15-20 minutes. Remove from oven and let stand for 5 minutes. Split in half by inserting a sharp knife next to the breast bone and pressing firmly, cut right down through the back bone.

MICROWAVE INSTRUCTIONS:

Rinse the hen and pat dry. Stuff with one of the stuffings suggested or your own. To give the bird a nice brown color, baste with a combination of 1 tsp.(5 mL) olive oil, ¼ tsp.(5 mL) paprika and ½ tsp.(2 mL) light soy sauce. Baste the underside first and roast, back side up, on **high** for 8 minutes on a rack in a baking dish. Turn over and baste, breast side up with the remaining mixture. Microwave at **high** 8 minutes more. Let stand for 5 minutes before splitting in half.

Yield: 2 servings

1 serving

		Food Groups
Calories	235	5 L Meat
Protein	37 g	
Total Fat	8 g	
Saturated Fat	3 g	
Carbohydrate	0 g	
Cholesterol	97 mg	
Sodium	114 mg	

Note: The above analysis does not include the stuffing of your choice. You will find stuffing recipes on pages 120-122. If you are using the microwave instructions, add 308 mg sodium, per serving, for the light soy sauce. This is the perfect little bird for two!

ROAST TURKEY BREAST

A cooking bag is used in this instance as it keeps the meat moist when the skin has been removed prior to cooking. The flour is a part of the instructions for the bag use and is not calculated into the nutrient analysis.

1½-2 lbs.	turkey breast roast	.8 kg
1	roasting bag	1
¼ tsp.	crushed savory	1 mL
1 tbsp.	flour	15 mL

Remove the skin and any visible fat from the turkey. Rub with savory. Follow the instructions that accompany the roasting bag to further prepare the roast. Roast in a pan in a 325°F (150°C) oven for 60 minutes. Let stand for 15-20 minutes after it has been removed from the oven. Remove the bones prior to placing the meat on a serving platter. It will then slice very nicely.

MICROWAVE INSTRUCTIONS:

Follow the above instructions to prepare the roast. Place the roasting bag in a microwave-safe dish. Microwave on **high** for 6 minutes, then reduce to **medium** for 12-14 minutes. Test for doneness. Allow to stand for 15 minutes. Remove the bones prior to placing the meat on a serving platter. This will make it easier to slice.

Yield: 4 servings

1 serving

Calories	157	Food Groups
Protein	30 g	4 L Meat
Total Fat	3 g	
Saturated Fat	1 g	
Carbohydrate	0 g	
Cholesterol	69 mg	
Sodium	63 mg	

Serving Suggestion: The Onion Cranberry Sauce, page 123, is a lovely change from gravy for this dish. Add all your favorites by way of potatoes, squash, etc. to make it into a festive meal.

TURKEY MEAT LOAF

8 oz.	ground turkey	225 g
½ cup	grated carrots	125 mL
1	egg white	1
2 tbsp.	minced onion	30 mL
¼ cup	dry red wine	60 mL
¼ tsp.	crushed oregano leaves	1 mL
¼ tsp.	salt	1 mL
1 tbsp.	wheat bran	15 mL

Combine all ingredients in a bowl and mix just until blended. Pack lightly into a 2-cup (500 mL) casserole that has been sprayed with a nonstick spray. Bake at 350°F (180°C) for 40 minutes. Let set for a few minutes before serving. Drain off any fat that accumulates. Individual portions may be made by baking in 4 muffin cups, sprayed with nonstick spray. Bake for only 20 minutes. Drain off any fat that accumulates. Serve 2 per person.

MICROWAVE INSTRUCTIONS:

Combine all ingredients in a bowl and mix just until blended. Pack lightly in a 2-cup (500 mL) microwave container that has been sprayed with a nonstick spray. Microwave on **medium** for 10 minutes, rotating at ½ time. Let stand for 5 minutes. Drain off any fat that accumulates.

Yield: 2 servings

1 serving

Calories	156	Food Groups
Protein	25 g	3 L Meat
Total Fat	3 g	
Saturated Fat	1 g	
Carbohydrate	4 g	
Cholesterol	69 mg	
Sodium	346 mg	

Note: This is a very low-calorie, low-fat entrée! You could take this opportunity to add a few extra calories and fat, (perhaps a favorite dessert?) and still keep the totals down.

Pasta, Casseroles & Stuffings

PASTA PRIMAVERA

1	small eggplant, peeled, diced	1
	salt	
2 tsp.	olive oil	10 mL
½ cup	chopped green pepper	125 mL
½ cup	chopped onion	125 mL
1	celery stalk, sliced	1
1	garlic clove, minced	1
2	medium tomatoes, chopped	2
1	small zucchini, diced	1
½ tsp.	crushed oregano leaves	2 mL
½ tsp.	crushed basil leaves	2 mL
	ground pepper to taste	
2 cups	cooked pasta	500 mL
2 tbsp.	grated Parmesan cheese	30 mL

Place eggplant in a colander, sprinkle with salt and set aside. Heat oil in frying pan. Add green pepper, onion, celery, garlic, tomatoes, zucchini and seasonings. Wash eggplant and add to frying pan. Cover and simmer, stirring frequently, until tender, about 10 minutes. Add cooked pasta to vegetables. Heat through. Sprinkle with cheese to serve.

MICROWAVE INSTRUCTIONS:

Prepare eggplant as above. Place oil in large microwave casserole. Add green pepper, onion, celery, garlic, tomatoes, zucchini and seasonings. Cover and microwave on **medium** for 1 minute. Wash eggplant and add to the casserole. Microwave on **medium** 5-7 minutes, or until tender. Add cooked pasta; microwave on **high** 1 minute to heat. Sprinkle with cheese to serve.

Yield: 2 servings

1 Serving

Calories	389	Food Groups
Protein	14 g	2 R Meat
Total Fat	8 g	4 Bread
Saturated Fat	2 g	2 Vegetables
Carbohydrate	70 g	
Cholesterol	4 mg	
Sodium	131 mg	

See photograph opposite.

Pasta Primavera, page 112

PASTA WITH VEGETABLE CLAM SAUCE

1	medium eggplant	1
½ cup	water	125 mL
1 cup	canned crushed tomatoes	250 mL
7 oz.	canned tomato sauce	200 mL
½ tsp.	crushed basil leaves	2 mL
½ tsp	crushed oregano leaves	2 mL
1	garlic clove, minced	1
¼ cup	chopped onions	60 mL
1 cup	sliced mushrooms	250 mL
½ cup	canned clams	125 mL
2 cups	cooked, drained pasta	500 mL
2 tbsp.	grated Parmesan cheese	30 mL

Cut ends off eggplant and peel. Dice into 1" (2 cm) cubes. Place in a large sauce-pan. Add ½ cup (125 mL) water and bring to a boil. Reduce heat and simmer, covered, for 15 minutes, or until almost soft. Drain off water. Add the next 7 ingredients. Stir the sauce and simmer for 10 minutes. Add the clams and heat through. Serve over cooked pasta, sprinkle with cheese.

MICROWAVE INSTRUCTIONS:

Cut the ends off eggplant and peel. Dice into 1" (2 cm) cubes. Place in a large microwave casserole with lid. Add ¼ cup (60 mL) water. Microwave on **high** for 10 minutes. Stir after 5 minutes. Drain off water. Add next 7 ingredients. Microwave on **medium** 8-10 minutes, uncovered. Stir every 2 minutes. Add clams. Microwave on **high** for 30 seconds, to heat clams. Serve over cooked pasta, sprinkle with cheese.

Yield: 2 servings

1 serving		Food Groups
Calories	378	3 L Meat
Protein	22 g	3 Bread
Total Fat	4 g	4 Vegetables
Saturated Fat	1 g	
Carbohydrate	67 g	
Cholesterol	35 mg	
Sodium	467 mg	

SALMON & MACARONI CASSEROLE

½ cup	raw macaroni	125 mL
2 cups	skim milk	500 mL
3 tbsp.	flour	45 mL
2 tbsp	minced onion	30 mL
¼ tsp.	white pepper	1 mL
1 tbsp.	grated horseradish	15 mL
¼ tsp.	Worcestershire sauce	1 mL
7.5 oz.	can pink salmon	213 g
½ cup	thinly sliced carrots	125 mL
1 cup	sliced fresh mushrooms	250 mL
1 oz.	skim milk cheese, grated	30 g
1 tbsp.	grated Parmesan cheese	15 mL

Cook macaroni as package directs, but only until barely tender. Rinse under cold water. Heat 1½ cups (375 mL) milk to the scalding point. Meanwhile, mix the flour with the remaining milk and beat to remove all lumps. Stir briskly into the hot milk and continue stirring over medium heat, until thickened and smooth. Add onion, pepper, horseradish and Worcestershire sauce. Drain the salmon and place it in a medium casserole, sprayed with a nonstick spray, and break it apart gently with a fork. Add the macaroni, carrots and mushrooms. Pour the sauce over and stir gently to combine. Mix the 2 cheeses together and sprinkle on top. Bake at 350°F (180°C) for 20 minutes. Let stand for 10 minutes before serving.

SALMON & MACARONI CASSEROLE (Cont'd.)

MICROWAVE INSTRUCTIONS:

Cook macaroni as package directs, but only until barely tender. Rinse under cold water. Heat 1½ cups (375 mL) milk in a large glass measure on **high** for 2 minutes. Meanwhile, combine the flour and remaining milk and beat until smooth. Whisk into the hot milk, microwave on **high** for 1 minute more, or until smooth and thickened. Whisk to remove any lumps. Stir in the onion, pepper, horseradish and Worcestershire sauce. Drain the salmon and place in a microwave-safe casserole, sprayed with a nonstick spray. Break salmon apart gently and combine with macaroni, carrots and mushrooms. Pour the sauce over and stir gently to combine. Mix the 2 cheeses together and sprinkle on top. Microwave on **medium** 5 minutes, or until heated through and bubbly. Let stand 5 minutes before serving.

Yield: 3 servings (save 1 for lunch the next day!)

1 Serving

		Food Groups
Calories	349	3 R Meat
Protein	27 g	1½ Bread
Fat	12 g	1 Vegetable
Saturated Fat	4 g	1 Milk
Carbohydrate	34 g	
Cholesterol	42 mg	
Sodium	518 mg	

Note: If you prefer, you may use canned tuna, which will reduce the fat content to 5 grams, the saturated fat to 1 g and total calories to 307 per serving.

CREAMY GARLIC SCALLOPS

2 tsp.	soft margarine or butter	10 mL
2	garlic cloves, minced	2
1	large green onion, sliced	1
7 oz.	fresh or frozen scallops	200 g
1 tbsp.	flour	15 mL
⅔ cup	skim milk	150 mL
⅓ cup	dry white wine	75 mL
2 cups	cooked pasta	500 mL
2 tbsp.	grated Parmesan cheese	30 mL

In a heavy frying pan, melt the margarine. Add the garlic and onion. Cook until limp over low heat. Raise heat to medium and add the scallops. Cut any large scallops in ½. Sauté for 3-4 minutes. Reduce heat to low; stir in the flour, mix completely. Stir in the milk slowly, then the wine. Continue to stir until sauce has thickened, about 5 minutes. Pour over pasta; sprinkle with Parmesan.

MICROWAVE INSTRUCTIONS:

Melt margarine in a casserole on **high** for 30 seconds. Add garlic and onion. Microwave on **high** 1 minute, or until onion is limp. Add scallops. Cover and microwave on **medium** 3 minutes, to cook scallops. Stir in flour and ½ the milk. Microwave, uncovered, on **medium** 1 minute. Stir; add remaining milk. Microwave on **medium** 1 minute, or until sauce has thickened and flour is cooked. Add the wine. Continue to microwave on **medium**, stirring every 30 seconds, until thickened. Pour over pasta; sprinkle with Parmesan.

Yield: 2 servings

1 Serving

		Food Groups
Calories	388	Food Groups
Protein	29 g	3 L Meat
Total Fat	7 g	1 Milk
Saturated Fat	2 g	2½ Bread
Carbohydrate	47 g	
Cholesterol	51 mg	
Sodium	374 mg	

Serving Suggestion: Serve a brightly colored, firm-textured vegetable such as asparagus spears, broccoli, baby beets, etc.

EUROPEAN SPATZLE

½ cup	flour	125 mL
⅛ tsp.	salt	0.5 mL
⅛ tsp.	ground sage	0.5 mL
¼ cup	water	60 mL
1	egg, slightly beaten	1

Bring 3-4 cups (750 mL-1 L) water to a boil on top of the stove. In the meantime, sift the flour, salt and sage together into a small bowl. Add the ¼ cup (60 mL) water to the beaten egg and mix well. Stir into the flour mixture until smooth. Do not beat. Drop, by pea-sized amounts, into the boiling water, off the tip of a spoon (it gets easier as you practice a bit). The spatzle will rise to the top. Do only 1 layer at a time. Cook 3 to 4 minutes, lift out with a slotted spoon and drain for a few seconds. Place in a serving bowl and keep warm while you prepare the rest. Before serving, mix the spatzle with a bit of butter or margarine. (The butter or margarine is not included in the analysis.)

MICROWAVE INSTRUCTIONS:

Microwave cooking is unacceptable for this recipe.

Yield: 2 servings

1 Serving

Calories	168	Food Groups
Protein	7 g	2 Bread
Total Fat	3 g	½ R Meat
Saturated Fat	1 g	
Carbohydrate	26 g	
Cholesterol	151 mg	
Sodium	134 mg	

Serving Suggestions: Spatzle is often served, instead of potatoes, with any meat that has been cooked in a sauce or has a gravy, such as pot roast, stews and, of course, with Chicken Paprika, page 101.

SIMPLE SUPPER CASSEROLE

2	medium tomatoes*	2
1 cup	whole kernel corn	250 mL
½	cooking onion, sliced and separated into rings	½
2	celery stalks, sliced in chunks	2
¼ cup	raw rice	60 mL
¼ tsp.	garlic powder	1 mL
1 tsp.	chili powder	5 mL
⅛ tsp.	white pepper	0.5 mL
6 oz.	low-fat mozzarella cheese, grated	180 g

*canned tomatoes may be used. You will then need ½ cup (125 mL) of the juice as well.

Coarsely chop the tomatoes. Combine all of the vegetables in a casserole. Add the rice, seasonings and ½ of the grated cheese. Stir well. Press down a bit. Sprinkle with the remaining cheese. Bake 30-40 minutes in a 350°F (180°C) oven. Add a bit of water if it starts to dry out.

MICROWAVE INSTRUCTIONS:

Coarsely chop the tomatoes. Combine all of the vegetables in a microwave casserole with a lid. Add the rice, seasonings and ½ of the grated cheese. Stir well. Press down a bit. Sprinkle with the remaining cheese. Cover and microwave on **medium** for15 minutes. Check rice for doneness. Add water if it is drying and microwave a few minutes more on **medium**, if necessary to cook rice.

Yield: 2 servings

1 Serving

Calories	448	**Food Groups**
Protein	28 g	3 R Meat
Total Fat	16 g	3 Bread
Saturated Fat	9 g	1 Vegetable
Carbohydrate	54 g	
Cholesterol	50 mg	
Sodium	459 mg	

Serving Suggestion: Serve with a salad.

PIE PLATE POTATO PIZZA

1	large thin-skinned potato	1
½ cup	canned tomatoes, diced	125 mL
4	large mushrooms, sliced thinly	4
2 tbsp.	minced onion	30 mL
¼ tsp.	crushed basil leaves	1 mL
¼ tsp.	crushed thyme	1 mL
1	small garlic clove, minced	1
5	stuffed green olives, sliced	5
5 oz.	low-fat mozzarella, grated	140 g

Spray a pie pan with nonstick spray. Slice potato about ¼" (1 cm) thick. Lay slices on the bottom of the pan, overlapping slightly and along the sides to form a "crust." Spray with nonstick spray. Bake at 400°F (200°C) for 40 minutes, until slightly browned and potatoes are cooked. Combine tomatoes, mushrooms, onion and seasonings. When crust is ready, spread with the mushroom mixture. Top with olives then cheese. Bake for 10 minutes.

MICROWAVE INSTRUCTIONS:

Prepare the crust as above, using a glass pie plate. Be sure the slices of potato hang over edge of plate slightly. Microwave on **high** for 5-6 minutes, turning the pan every 2 minutes until potatoes are almost soft. Place in the conventional oven about 5" (12 cm) away from the broiler and broil for 5 minutes, or until edges are drying and the potatoes are starting to brown. Remove. Combine the tomatoes, mushrooms, onion and seasonings. When the crust is ready, spread with mushroom mixture. Top with olives then cheese. Cover with plastic wrap; microwave on **medium** for 3-4 minutes, turning frequently, until cheese is melted and bubbly.

Yield: 2 servings

1 serving

Calories	295	**Food Groups**
Protein	21 g	3 L Meat
Total Fat	14 g	1 Bread
Saturated Fat	8 g	1 Vegetable
Carbohydrate	22 g	
Cholesterol	42 mg	
Sodium	804 mg	

APPLE STUFFING

1	green onion, sliced	1
1	small apple, cored and diced	1
1 tbsp.	raisins	15 mL
2 tbsp.	orange juice	30 mL
½ tsp.	prepared mustard	2 mL
¼ tsp.	summer savory	1 mL
	pepper to taste	
½	bread slice, cubed	½

Combine first 7 ingredients in a small frying pan and cook over low heat until the apple is tender. Toss with the cubed bread and use as stuffing for Cornish Hen, page 108, or bake in a small casserole, sprayed with nonstick spray, for 10 minutes at 350°F (180°C).

MICROWAVE INSTRUCTIONS:

Combine first 7 ingredients in a small casserole with a lid. Cover and microwave on **high** for 3 minutes, or until apple is tender. Toss with cubed bread and use to stuff Cornish Hen or microwave in a small casserole, sprayed with a nonstick spray, for 4-5 minutes on **medium**.

Yield: 2 servings

1 Serving

Calories	72	Food Groups
Protein	1 g	1 Fruit
Total Fat	0 g	½ Bread
Saturated Fat	0 g	
Carbohydrate	17 g	
Cholesterol	0 mg	
Sodium	46 mg	

WILD RICE STUFFING

1 cup	water	250 mL
2 tbsp.	wild rice, washed, drained	30 mL
2 tbsp.	brown rice	30 mL
1 tbsp.	chopped onion	15 mL
¼ tsp.	ground nutmeg	1 mL
⅛ tsp.	pepper	0.5 mL

Bring water to a boil in a small saucepan with a lid. Add all other ingredients; cover and simmer about 40 minutes, or until rice is tender and all liquid is absorbed.

MICROWAVE INSTRUCTIONS:

In a deep casserole with a lid, combine all ingredients. Cover and microwave on **high** for 3 minutes; reduce to **medium** for 30-40 minutes, or until rice is tender and liquid is absorbed.

Yield: 2 servings

1 Serving

Calories	108	Food Groups
Protein	3 g	1½ Bread
Total Fat	0 g	
Saturated Fat	0 g	
Carbohydrate	23 g	
Cholesterol	0 mg	
Sodium	2 mg	

Serving Suggestion: Use to stuff the Cornish Game Hen, page 108, or as a side dish for any plain meat.

BARLEY STUFFING

1 cup	water	250 mL
¼ cup	pot or pearl barley	60 mL
1 tbsp.	Parmesan cheese	15 mL
1 tbsp.	chopped onion	15 mL
1 tbsp.	chopped green onion	15 mL
1	garlic clove, minced	1
¼ tsp.	ground sage	1 mL

Combine all ingredients in a small saucepan. Cover and bring to a boil, reduce heat and simmer until the barley is tender, about 40 minutes. Use to stuff Cornish Game Hen, page 108, or double the recipe and stuff a small chicken.

MICROWAVE INSTRUCTIONS:

Combine all ingredients in a deep casserole with a lid. Cover and microwave on **high** for 3 minutes then reduce to **medium** for 20-25 minutes, or until barley is tender.

Yield: 2 servings

1 Serving

Calories	96	Food Groups	
Protein	3 g	1 Bread	
Total Fat	1 g		
Saturated Fat	1 g		
Carbohydrate	19 g		
Cholesterol	2 mg		
Sodium	51 mg		

ONION CRANBERRY SAUCE

½ cup	sliced onion	125 mL
½ cup	orange juice	125 mL
1 cup	fresh cranberries	250 mL
½ cup	white wine	125 mL
1	garlic clove, minced	1
2 tbsp.	brown sugar	30 mL
¼ tsp.	crushed oregano leaves	1 mL
¼ tsp.	crushed savory leaves	1 mL

Combine all ingredients in a saucepan. Stir and cover. Bring to a boil. Reduce heat and simmer for 20-30 minutes. Stir every 5 minutes.

MICROWAVE INSTRUCTIONS:

Combine all ingredients in a deep casserole with a lid. Cover and microwave on **high** for 4 minutes. Reduce to **low** and continue to microwave 5 minutes more, or until cranberries are soft. Stir every 2 minutes.

Yield: 4 servings

1 Serving

Calories	72	Food Groups
Protein	1 g	1 Fruit
Total Fat	0 g	
Saturated Fat	0 g	
Carbohydrate	15 g	
Cholesterol	0 mg	
Sodium	4 mg	

Serving Suggestions: A low-fat alternative to gravy to accompany your roast turkey breast, page 109. This sauce is lovely with chicken or any leftover plain meats. Just heat and serve.

NOTES

Salads & Salad Dressings

SUMMER TOMATO SALAD

1	medium tomato	1
1	onion slice, in rings	1
1 tbsp.	low-calorie Italian dressing	15 mL
½ tsp.	olive oil	2 mL
½ tsp.	granulated sugar	2 mL

Wash tomato. Slice into a bowl. Add onion. Combine dressing with oil and sugar. Pour over tomato slices and onion. Let stand for a few minutes, at room temperature, before serving.

Yield: 2 servings

1 Serving

Calories	42	Food Groups	
Protein	1 g	1 Vegetable	
Total Fat	2 g		
Saturated Fat	0 g		
Carbohydrate	6 g		
Cholesterol	5 mg		
Sodium	112 mg		

Note: Use Bermuda or Spanish onion for the best flavor.

BASIC SALAD DRESSING

1 cup	olive oil	250 mL
⅓ cup	wine vinegar	75 mL
½ cup	water	125 mL
2 tbsp.	granulated sugar	30 mL
1	garlic clove, minced	1
1 tbsp.	onion juice	15 mL
¼ tsp.	salt	1 mL
1 tsp.	dry mustard	5 mL
1 tsp.	poppy seeds	5 mL
½ tsp.	dried tarragon leaves	2 mL

In blender jar, combine all ingredients and blend for 30 seconds. This may also be made with a hand mixer in a deep bowl or measuring cup.

Yield: 28 servings of 1 tbsp. each

126

BASIC SALAD DRESSING
(Cont'd.)

1 serving

Calories	82	Food Groups
Protein	0 g	1½ Fat
Fat	9 g	
Saturated Fat	1 g	
Carbohydrate	1 g	
Cholesterol	0 mg	
Sodium	69 mg	

Note: This is an excellent source of mono-unsaturated fats.

CUCUMBERS IN YOGURT & SOUR CREAM

¼ tsp.	dillweed	1 mL
¼ tsp.	garlic powder	1 mL
¼ tsp	salt	1 mL
1 tsp.	lemon juice	5 mL
⅛ tsp.	white pepper	0.5 mL
⅓ cup	low-fat yogurt	75 mL
⅓ cup	low-fat sour cream	75 mL
¾ cup	sliced cucumbers	175 mL
	lettuce cups	
	sliced radish for garnish	

Combine first 7 ingredients. Fold in cucumbers and chill. Serve in lettuce cups. Garnish with thin slices of radishes.

Yield: 2 servings

1 Serving

Calories	44	Food Groups
Protein	2 g	1 Vegetable
Total Fat	2 g	
Saturated Fat	1 g	
Carbohydrate	4 g	
Cholesterol	12 mg	
Sodium	212 mg	

Serving Suggestion: Use to accompany a spicy meal.

TABBOULI

⅓ cup	bulgar wheat	75 mL
⅔ cup	cold water	150 mL
1 tbsp.	olive oil	15 mL
3 tbsp.	lemon juice	45 mL
¼ tsp.	salt	1 mL
¼ tsp.	pepper	1 mL
¼ cup	chopped fresh parsley	60 mL
2 tsp.	chopped fresh mint OR 1 tsp.	10 mL
	(5 mL) dried mint flakes	5 mL
2	green onions, chopped	2
1	small tomato, diced	1
	romaine lettuce	

Soak the bulgar in cold water for an hour. Drain well and squeeze out excess liquid in a towel. Combine oil, lemon juice, salt and pepper and shake well. Add remaining ingredients, except romaine, to bulgar. Pour dressing over and toss to mix well. If time permits, allow to stand for 1 hour to blend flavors. Serve as a salad on small inner romaine lettuce leaves.

Yield: 4 servings

1 Serving

Calories	76	**Food Groups**
Protein	1 g	½ Bread
Total Fat	4 g	½ Fat
Saturated Fat	1 g	
Carbohydrate	9 g	
Cholesterol	0 mg	
Sodium	129 mg	

CHILI BEAN SALAD

This supper salad gets better as it sets, so we gave you enough for another meal or for lunches. It also travels well.

1 tsp.	chili powder	5 mL
½ tbsp.	olive oil	7 mL
2 tbsp.	vinegar	30 mL
1 tbsp.	water	15 mL
1 tsp.	sugar	5 mL
2 tsp.	tomato ketchup	10 mL
19 oz.	can kidney beans (not drained)	540 mL
½ cup	diced green pepper	125 mL
½ cup	diced Spanish onion	125 mL
8 oz.	low-fat mozzarella cheese, cubed	225 g

In a small saucepan, heat the chili powder in the olive oil. Remove from heat and add the vinegar, water, sugar and ketchup. Stir well. Combine the remaining ingredients in a bowl. Pour sauce over vegetables and stir well, to coat. Cover and refrigerate 1 hour or more. To serve, mound in lettuce cups.

MICROWAVE INSTRUCTIONS:

In a microwave-safe container heat the chili powder in the olive oil by microwaving on **high** for 30 seconds. Add the vinegar, water, sugar and ketchup. Stir well. Combine the remaining ingredients in a bowl. Pour sauce over vegetables and stir well. Cover and refrigerate 1 hour or more.

Yield: 4 servings

1 Serving

		Food Groups
Calories	336	
Protein	22 g	3 R Meat
Total Fat	16 g	2 Bread
Saturated Fat	7 g	
Carbohydrate	28 g	
Cholesterol	33 mg	
Sodium	312 mg	

Serving Suggestion: Surround with sliced tomatoes and cucumbers. Pass bread sticks or plain tortilla chips.

JELLIED POTATO SALAD

1½ tsp.	plain gelatin	7 mL
2 tbsp.	cold water	30 mL
½ cup	boiling water	125 mL
1 cup	diced cooked potato	250 mL
1	green onion, chopped	1
2 oz.	chopped ham	60 g
2 oz.	low-fat mozzarella cheese, diced	60 g
1	hard-cooked egg, diced	1
1 tsp.	vinegar	5 mL
⅛ tsp	white pepper	0.5 mL
¼ tsp.	celery seed	1 mL
1 tbsp.	calorie-reduced mayonnaise	15 mL
½ tsp.	prepared mustard	2 mL
2 tbsp.	low-fat yogurt	30 mL
	sliced cucumber for garnish	

Soak gelatin in cold water for 2 minutes. Add boiling water and stir to dissolve gelatin. Chill until it becomes the consistency of egg white. Combine potatoes, onion, ham, cheese and egg. In a separate bowl mix vinegar, pepper, celery seed, mayonnaise, mustard and yogurt. Add to potato mixture, and toss to coat well. Beat gelatin mixture until fluffy. Combine with potato mixture and pour into 2-3-cup (500-750 mL) mold or bowl. Chill to set. Unmold and garnish with sliced cucmber on lettuce leaves.

Yield: 2 servings

1 Serving

		Food Groups
Calories	260	
Protein	18 g	2 R Meat
Total Fat	14 g	1 Bread
Saturated Fat	6 g	1 Fat
Carbohydrate	17 g	
Cholesterol	165 mg	
Sodium	546 mg	

Serving Suggestion: This is a terrific picnic item. So easy to keep chilled. Just take along a few bread sticks and a raw vegetable for munching.

CRAB SALAD

4	canned artichoke hearts	4
6 oz.	crab meat or mock crab	180 g
1	small ripe tomato	1
2 cups	torn lettuce leaves	500 mL
	lettuce cups	
4	lemon slices for garnish	4
	parsley sprigs for garnish	

DRESSING:

2 tbsp.	reduced-calorie mayonnaise	30 mL
¼ cup	low-fat yogurt	60 mL
2	stuffed olives, chopped	2
2 tsp.	minced green or red pepper	10 mL
1 tsp.	minced green onion	5 mL
1 tsp.	chili sauce	5 mL
1 tsp.	lemon juice	5 mL

Chill all salad ingredients. Cut the artichoke hearts into bite-sized pieces. Flake the crab meat. Cut the tomato into 8 wedges. In a medium-sized bowl, combine the lettuce, artichoke hearts, crab and 4 of the tomato wedges (reserve the other 4 for garnish). Combine all of the dressing ingredients and pour over the salad. Toss gently, just to combine. Place 2 lettuce cups on serving plates. Divide the salad between the 2 plates. Garnish each with the remaining tomato wedges, parsley sprigs and 2 lemon twists.

Yield: 2 servings

1 Serving

Calories	144	Food Groups
Protein	13 g	2 L Meat
Total Fat	6 g	2 Vegetables
Saturated Fat	1 g	
Carbohydrate	10 g	
Cholesterol	61 mg	
Sodium	411 mg	

Serving Suggestion: Match this up with some fresh whole wheat rolls and you have a quick summer luncheon.

HOT SEAFOOD SALAD

5 oz.	crab meat or mock crab	150 g
3 oz.	cooked, deveined shrimp	90 g
¼ cup	chopped green pepper	60 mL
¼ cup	chopped red pepper	60 mL
1	green onion, sliced	1
2 tbsp.	reduced-calorie mayonnaise	30 mL
3 tbsp.	low-fat yogurt	45 mL
¼ tsp	Worcestershire sauce	1 mL
2	lettuce leaves	2
1½ cups	chow mein noodles	375 mL
	lemon wedges for garnish	

Break crab meat into bite-sized pieces. If shrimp are large, cut in half, otherwise leave whole. In a bowl, place crab and shrimp; add peppers and onion. Combine mayonnaise, yogurt and Worcestershire sauce. Pour over seafood mixture and mix, just until ingredients are coated with the dressing. Place in an ovenproof dish that has been sprayed with nonstick spray. Bake in a 350°F (180°C) oven for 20 minutes. Place large lettuce leaf on a plate, top with half the chow mein noodles. Ladle half the baked seafood over noodles, garnish with lemon wedges. Repeat with the second plate. Serve immediately.

MICROWAVE INSTRUCTIONS:

Prepare ingredients as above to the point of baking. Place salad in a microwave casserole, sprayed with a nonstick spray. Microwave at **medium** for 5 to 6 minutes, rotating at half time. Place large lettuce leaf on a plate, top with half the chow mein noodles. Ladle half the baked seafood over noodles. Garnish with lemon wedges. Repeat. Serve immediately.

Yield: 2 servings

1 Serving

Calories	320	**Food Groups**
Protein	24 g	3 R Meat
Total Fat	13 g	1½ Bread
Saturated Fat	3 g	
Carbohydrate	25 g	
Cholesterol	117 mg	
Sodium	505 mg	

TROPICAL SALMON SALAD

7.5 oz.	can red or pink salmon	213 g
½	fresh fruit, diced (we used ½ mango, peeled)	½
1 tbsp.	calorie-reduced mayonnaise	15 mL
3 tbsp.	low-fat yogurt	45 mL
1 tbsp.	pickle relish	15 mL
½ tsp.	prepared mustard	2 mL
1 cup	shredded lettuce or lettuce cups	250 mL
	lemon wedges for garnish	

Drain salmon, remove bones and skin. Break into bite-sized pieces. Place in a bowl with the diced fruit of your choice. Blend mayonnaise, yogurt, relish and mustard and mix lightly with salmon and fruit. Chill for 1 hour. Mound salad mixture in lettuce cups or on shredded lettuce arranged on serving plates. Garnish with lemon wedges.

Yield: 2 servings

1 Serving

		Food Groups
Calories	219	
Protein	15 g	2 R Meat
Total Fat	12 g	1 Fat
Saturated Fat	3 g	1 Fruit
Carbohydrate	12 g	
Cholesterol	25 mg	
Sodium	320 mg	

Serving Suggestion: This is lovely with a muffin, bread sticks, or Bran Bread, page 61. Fresh salmon, poached, may be used in place of canned salmon.

TUNA APPLE SALAD

2 cups	torn lettuce	500 mL
6 oz.	can tuna, well drained	184 g
½ cup	pineapple chunks, unsweetened	125 mL
1	small apple, diced	1
¼ cup	calorie-reduced mayonnaise	60 mL
½ tsp.	salt-reduced soy sauce	2 mL
½ tsp	lemon juice	2 mL
1 tbsp	pineapple juice	15 mL
2 tbsp.	chopped walnuts, pecans or almonds	30 mL

Place lettuces (2 or 3 kinds are nice, if you have them), in a medium-sized bowl. Break the tuna into chunks and add to lettuce, along with pineapple and apple. In a small bowl, combine mayonnaise, soy sauce, lemon juice and pineapple juice. Pour over salad and toss lightly until well coated. (Maybe refrigerated for 30 minutes or so at this point, to chill completely.) Spoon into lettuce cups on salad plates and sprinkle with nuts.

Yield: 2 servings

1 Serving

		Food Groups
Calories	318	
Protein	22 g	3 L Meat
Total Fat	15 g	1½ Fat
Saturated Fat	2 g	2 Fruit
Carbohydrate	24 g	
Cholesterol	47 mg	
Sodium	677 mg	

Serving Suggestion: Lovely with a nice fresh bun from the bakery or the Whole Wheat Scones, page 59. Cooked chicken would substitute nicely for the tuna, if you desire.

CHICKEN PASTA SALAD

1½ cups	cooked pasta, rotini, shells, etc.	375 mL
6 oz.	cooked chicken, shredded	180 g
½ cup	canned artichoke hearts	125 mL
½ cup	diced celery	125 mL
1	medium tomato, diced OR 6-8 cherry tomatoes cut in halves	1
1	green onion, sliced	1
¼ cup	low-calorie Italian dressing	60 mL
1 tbsp.	olive oil	15 mL
	lettuce leaves	
	assorted raw vegetables for garnish	

Combine first 6 ingredients in a large bowl and toss lightly. Mix the Italian dressing and olive oil and pour over salad. Toss again and chill for at least 2 hours, for flavors to blend. Serve in lettuce cups and garnish with a variety of raw vegetables, cucumber slices, radish roses, broccoli and/or cauliflower pieces.

Yield: 2 servings

1 Serving

Calories	359	**Food Groups**
Protein	29 g	3 L Meat
Total Fat	12 g	2 Bread
Saturated Fat	2 g	1 Vegetable
Carbohydrate	33 g	1 Fat
Cholesterol	67 mg	
Sodium	599 mg	

Note: This is a high sodium meal because of the salad dressing. You might want to eat lower sodium foods the rest of the day.

ITALIAN SUPPER SALAD

2 cups	torn lettuce	500 mL
2 oz.	low-fat mozzarella cheese sliced in thin strips	60 g
½ cup	chick-peas	125 mL
2 oz.	very dry salami, sliced in thin strips	60 g
¼ cup	diced green pepper	60 mL
½ cup	sliced celery	125 mL
1	green onion, sliced	1
¼ cup	low-calorie Italian dressing	60 mL
2 tsp.	olive oil	10 mL
1	hard-cooked egg	1
1	medium tomato, cut into 8 wedges	1

Combine the first 7 ingredients in a large bowl. Mix the salad dressing with the olive oil and pour over. Toss gently to mix. Divide onto 2 serving plates. Slice the hard-cooked egg and garnish each salad with half of the egg, plus half of the tomato wedges.

Yield: 2 servings

1 serving

Calories	351	Food Groups
Protein	20 g	3 R Meat
Total Fat	21 g	1 Bread
Saturated Fat	7 g	2 Vegetables
Carbohydrate	23 g	1 Fat
Cholesterol	146 mg	
Sodium	919 mg	

Note: While this meal is higher in fat and sodium than our usual fare, it is so easy to put together and tastes so good on a hot summer night, we wanted to include it for you. Serve with hot crusty rolls. Fat and sodium could be reduced at other meals to keep them under control for the day.

Vegetables

PEAS WITH WATER CHESTNUTS

¾ cup	cooked peas	175 mL
¼ cup	sliced water chestnuts	60 mL
½ tsp.	margarine or butter	2 mL

Cook peas as usual. **Do not drain.** Add the chestnuts and heat 1 minute. Drain and add the margarine. Mix well.

MICROWAVE INSTRUCTIONS:

Microwave peas in a small casserole with 2 tbsp. (30 mL) water on **high** for 4 minutes. Add the chestnuts and microwave 1 minute more. Drain and add the margarine. Mix well.

Yield: 2 servings

1 Serving

Calories	63	**Food Groups**
Protein	4 g	2 Vegetables
Total Fat	1 g	
Saturated Fat	0 g	
Carbohydrate	10 g	
Cholesterol	0 mg	
Sodium	188 mg	

STEAMED ZUCCHINI AND TOMATOES

2	small zucchini	2
2 tbsp.	water	30 mL
1	garlic clove, minced	1
⅛ tsp.	salt	0.5 mL
⅛ tsp.	pepper	0.5 mL
1	medium tomato, cut into ⅛'s	1
1 tsp.	olive oil	5 mL

Scrub zucchini, cut off ends and slice into ½" (1.3 cm) thick slices. Place in a small saucepan with 2 tbsp.(30 mL) water. Add the garlic, salt and pepper. Cover and cook over high heat for 1 minute then turn down to medium, add the tomatoes and steam 1-2 minutes more. Do not overcook. Drain well and toss gently with 1 tsp. (5 mL) olive oil.

MICROWAVE INSTRUCTIONS:

Prepare zucchini as above. Place in a microwave casserole with a lid. Add 1 tbsp (15 mL) water, garlic, salt and pepper. Cover and microwave on **high** for 1 minute. Add the tomato wedges and microwave on **high** 1 minute more. Drain off any liquid, toss gently with 1 tsp. (5 mL) olive oil.

Yield: 2 servings

1 Serving		
Calories	64	**Food Groups**
Protein	2 g	1 Vegetable
Total Fat	3 g	½ Fat
Saturated Fat	0 g	
Carbohydrate	9 mg	
Cholesterol	0 mg	
Sodium	123 mg	

Variations: This recipe works equally well substituting broccoli or cauliflower florets for the zucchini. The cooking time will be slightly longer for both, as zucchini cooks very quickly.

BROILED TOMATOES

1	medium tomato, cut in half	1
½ tsp.	margarine or butter	2 mL
¼ tsp.	crushed basil leaves	1 mL
¼ tsp.	crushed oregano leaves	1 mL

Place tomato halves on a baking sheet. Dab margarine on each and sprinkle with the basil and oregano. Place under the broiler, 5" (13 cm) away from the element, and broil just 1-2 minutes, until bubbly and tomato is heated through. This is a lovely summer vegetable.

MICROWAVE INSTRUCTIONS:

Prepare as above. Microwave on high for 1-2 minutes until tomato is heated through.

Yield: 2 servings

1 Serving

Calories	24	Food Groups
Protein	1 g	1 Vegetable
Total Fat	1 g	
Saturated Fat	0 g	
Carbohydrate	3 g	
Cholesterol	0 mg	
Sodium	19 mg	

See photograph page 80A.

SCALLOPED TOMATOES

1 cup	canned tomatoes	250 mL
1	celery stalk, sliced	1
1	small green onion, thinly sliced	1
1 tsp.	sugar	5 mL
¼ tsp.	crushed basil leaves	1 mL
½ cup	croutons	125 mL

Combine the vegetables and seasonings. Simmer, on top of the stove, for 10 minutes, or until celery is cooked. Spoon into 2 serving dishes and top each with half of the croutons.

MICROWAVE INSTRUCTIONS:

Combine the vegetables and seasonings in a microwave-safe container. Cover loosely. Microwave on **high** for 4-5 minutes, or until vegetables are cooked. Rotate at half time. Spoon into 2 serving dishes and top each with half of the croutons.

Yield: 2 servings

1 Serving

Calories	70	**Food Groups**
Protein	2 g	2 Vegetables
Total Fat	1 g	
Saturated Fat	0 g	
Carbohydrate	15 g	
Cholesterol	0 mg	
Sodium	227 mg	

141

SAVORY RICE

1 tsp.	soft margarine or butter	5 mL
¼ tsp.	garlic powder	1 mL
¼ tsp.	curry powder	1 mL
⅓ cup	raw white rice	75 mL
1 cup	chicken broth	250 mL
1 tbsp.	chopped fresh parsley	15 mL

In a small frying pan, melt the margarine. Add the garlic powder, curry powder and rice. Cook at low heat until the rice starts to brown. Add chicken broth and bring to a boil. Simmer for 20 minutes, or until the broth is absorbed. Stir in the parsley and let stand, covered, for 5 minutes.

MICROWAVE INSTRUCTIONS:

Put the margarine in a small casserole with a lid. Cover and microwave on **high** for 15 seconds, to melt margarine. Add garlic powder, curry powder and rice. Stir and cover. Microwave on **high** 1 minute. Add chicken broth and microwave on **high** for 4 minutes. Reduce to **medium** for 10 to 12 minutes more, or until liquid is absorbed. Stir in parsley and let stand 5 minutes.

Yield: 2 servings

1 Serving

Calories	133	**Food Groups**	
Protein	2 g	1½ Bread	
Total Fat	2 g	½ Fat	
Saturated Fat	0 g		
Carbohydrate	25 g		
Cholesterol	0 mg		
Sodium	501 mg		

Serving Suggestion: This will add zip and color to a plain meat meal.

See photograph page 80A.

COUSCOUS

This Moroccan staple is available in most supermarkets, in the specialty foods, or perhaps the pasta aisle. A pleasant change from potatoes.

¾ cup	water	175 mL
⅓ cup	couscous	75 mL
⅓ cup	diced celery	75 mL
¼ cup	sliced green onion	60 mL
2 tbsp.	coarsely chopped pecans	30 mL

Bring water to a boil in a small saucepan. Stir in couscous, celery and onion. Cover. Remove from the stove and let stand for 5 minutes. Fluff with a fork and add the pecans.

MICROWAVE INSTRUCTIONS:

Place the water in a casserole with a lid. Cover and microwave on **high** for 1 minute, or until it boils. Add couscous, celery and onion. Cover with lid or plastic wrap. Let stand for 5 minutes. Fluff with a fork and add the pecans.

Yield: 2 servings

1 Serving

Calories	98	**Food Groups**
Protein	3 g	1 Bread
Total Fat	1 g	1 Vegetable
Saturated Fat	0 g	
Carbohydrate	20 g	
Cholesterol	0 mg	
Sodium	8 mg	

Serving Suggestion: Terrific with the Fiery Lamb Broil, on page 82.

TURNIP & CARROT BAKE

1	medium turnip, peeled & diced	1
6	small carrots	6
¼ cup	chopped onion	60 mL
1 tbsp.	soft margarine or butter	15 mL
¼ tsp.	ground ginger	1 mL

Place turnip in a heavy saucepan with 1 cup (250 mL) water. Bring to a boil and simmer for 20 minutes. Peel and cut carrots into ¼" (1 cm) rounds. Add to turnips at the end of the 20 minutes, along with the onion. Continue to cook another 20 minutes, or until vegetables are soft. Drain, reserving the cooking water, place in a blender or food processor and process until smooth, adding a bit of the cooking water if necessary. Pour into a small casserole, sprayed with nonstick spray. Stir in the margarine and ginger. Bake at 350°F (180°C) for 10 minutes, to heat through.

MICROWAVE INSTRUCTIONS:

Place turnip in a casserole with lid, add ¼ cup (60 mL) water and microwave on **high** for 20 minutes. Meanwhile, peel and cut carrots in ¼" (1 cm) rounds. Add carrots and onion to turnips and microwave on **high** for 10 minutes more, or until vegetables are soft. Drain, reserving the cooking water, and place in a blender or food processor, process until smooth, adding a bit of the cooking water if necessary. Pour into a small casserole, sprayed with nonstick spray. Stir in the margarine and ginger. Microwave, covered, on **medium** for 3 minutes.

Yield: 6 servings

1 serving

Calories	49	Food Groups
Protein	1 g	1 Vegetable
Total Fat	2 g	
Saturated Fat	0 g	
Carbohydrate	8 g	
Cholesterol	0 mg	
Sodium	63 mg	

Note: This dish freezes very well. Reheat in the microwave. Drain as needed.

PARSNIP AND CARROT SWIRL

1	medium parsnip	1
1	medium carrot	1
½ cup	water	125 mL
1 tsp.	margarine or butter	5 mL
1 tbsp.	chopped fresh parsley	15 mL
⅛ tsp.	black pepper	0.5 mL

Wash and peel the parsnip and carrot and cut into small pieces. Place in a saucepan with ½ cup (125 mL) water. Bring to a boil and simmer for approximately 20 minutes, or until soft. Drain and place in blender or food processor. Purée until smooth. Remove to a serving dish and stir in remaining ingredients. Serve immediately or (this dish may be made ahead to this point) place in a casserole sprayed with nonstick spray, refrigerate, and reheat at serving time.

MICROWAVE INSTRUCTIONS:

Wash and peel the parsnip and carrot and cut into small pieces. Place in a microwave casserole with about ¼ cup (60 mL) water. Cover and microwave on **high** for 8 minutes. Stir at half time. Drain and place in blender or food processor. Purée until smooth. Remove to a serving dish and stir in remaining ingredients. Serve at once or (this dish may be made ahead to this point) place in a casserole sprayed with nonstick spray, refrigerate, and reheat in the microwave at serving time.

Yield: 2 servings

1 Serving

Calories	91	**Food Groups**
Protein	1 g	2 Vegetables
Total Fat	2 g	
Saturated Fat	0 g	
Carbohydrate	17 g	
Cholesterol	0 mg	
Sodium	48 mg	

Serving Suggestion: This goes nicely with the Roast Cornish Game Hen, page 108.

GLAZED CARROTS

1 cup	cooked carrots	250 mL
¼ cup	crushed pineapple	60 mL
2 tsp.	brown sugar	10 mL
½ tsp.	soft margarine or butter	2 mL

Combine all ingredients in a saucepan or frying pan. Heat, stirring gently until sauce is bubbly and shiny, about 5 minutes. Serve at once.

MICROWAVE INSTRUCTIONS:

Combine all ingredients in a microwave casserole. Cover and microwave on **high** 3 minutes, or until sauce is bubbly and shiny. Stir every minute. Serve at once.

Yield: 2 servings

1 Serving

Calories	80	**Food Groups**	
Protein	1 g	1 Vegetable	
Total Fat	1 g	½ Fruit	
Saturated Fat	0 g	1 tsp. sugar	
Carbohydrate	18 g		
Cholesterol	0 mg		
Sodium	64 mg		

HOT PICKLED BEETS

1 cup	sliced cooked beets	250 mL
2 tbsp.	sugar	30 mL
¼ cup	lemon juice	60 mL
½ tbsp.	cornstarch	7 mL

In a saucepan, combine the beets, sugar and 3 tbsp. (45 mL) of the lemon juice. Heat slowly and bring to a boil. Combine the cornstarch with the remaining lemon juice and stir into the beets. Stir until thickened and clear, about 1 minute.

MICROWAVE INSTRUCTIONS:

In a deep casserole with a lid, combine the beets, sugar and 3 tbsp. (45 mL) of the lemon juice. Microwave on **high** for 3 minutes. Combine the cornstarch and remaining lemon juice. Stir into beets. Microwave on high 30 seconds longer, or until thick and clear, stirring every 15 seconds.

Yield: 2 servings

1 Serving

Calories	96	Food Groups
Protein	1 g	1 Vegetable
Total Fat	0 g	3 tsp. sugar
Saturated Fat	0 g	
Carbohydrate	24 g	
Cholesterol	0 mg	
Sodium	222 mg	

Serving Suggestion: This is lovely with the Crispy Sesame Fillets, page 92.

LOW-FAT HOME FRIES

2	medium potatoes, scrubbed	2
1	small onion	1
¼ tsp.	salt	1 mL
¼ tsp.	pepper	1 mL

Spray a heavy frying pan with nonstick spray. Slice the potatoes as thinly as possible. Lay in a layer in the frying pan. Place any extra slices on top. Slice the onion into thin slices and separate into rings. Add to frying pan, along with salt and pepper. Fry, **uncovered**, about 5 minutes over medium heat. **Cover** and continue for another 5 minutes. Spray the potatoes with the nonstick spray, turn them over. Continue to fry 5 minutes, **uncovered**, then 5 minutes **covered**. When potatoes and onions are cooked they are ready to serve. They should be crisp on the outside and soft inside.

Yield: 2 servings

1 Serving

Calories	94	**Food Groups**	
Protein	3 g	1½ Bread	
Total Fat	0 g		
Saturated Fat	0 g		
Carbohydrate	21 g		
Cholesterol	0 mg		
Sodium	245 mg		

&

Desserts

CHERRY ALMOND TORTE

½ cup	finely chopped almonds	125 mL
⅔ cup	vanilla wafer crumbs	150 mL
14 oz.	can pitted bing cherries	398 mL
2 tbsp.	kirsch (optional)	30 mL
6	egg whites	6
3 tbsp.	granulated sugar	45 mL
6	egg yolks	6
2 tbsp.	granulated sugar	30 mL
3 tbsp.	lemon juice	45 mL
¼ tsp.	salt	1 mL
3	egg whites	3
3 tbsp.	brown sugar	45 mL
2 tbsp.	sliced almonds	30 mL

In a small bowl, combine chopped almonds and vanilla wafer crumbs. Set a side. Drain cherries thoroughly, squeezing gently with the back of a spoon. If using kirsch add to cherries and set aside. In a large bowl, beat egg whites until frothy. Gradually add the **first** amount of sugar, beating well after each addition. Beat until soft peaks form and whites do not slide when bowl is tipped. In another bowl, beat egg yolks, **second** amount of sugar, lemon juice and salt until thick and lemon colored. Gently spread egg yolk mixture over the egg whites. Spoon ¼ of the almond crumb mixture on top and gently fold in, with a few strokes, until batter is only **partially** blended. Repeat with second and third portions of crumbs, then spoon remaining mixture over batter and fold until **just** blended. Do not overmix! Turn batter into a 9" or 10" (22-25 cm) springform pan and spread to edges. Drain cherries and place evenly over batter. Bake at 350°F (180°C) for 30-40 minutes, or until torte is done. (Insert a toothpick, if it comes out clean with no batter clinging to it, it is done.) Cool in pan, on a rack, for 15 minutes. Remove side rim and cut away from pan bottom, if desired. When cooled, place torte on a baking sheet

CHERRY ALMOND TORTE
(Cont'd.)

Meringue: Beat the egg whites, gradually adding the brown sugar, until soft peaks form. Cover top and sides of torte with meringue. Sprinkle top with sliced almonds. Bake at 350°F (180°C) 10-15 minutes, or until golden brown. Cool. Before cutting each serving, dip knife blade into hot water.

Yield: 10 servings

1 Serving

Calories	233	Food Groups
Protein	8 g	1 Bread
Total Fat	11 g	1 R Meat
Saturated Fat	2 g	1 Fat
Carbohydrate	28 g	3 tsp. sugar
Cholestrol	181 mg	
Sodium	132 mg	

Serving Suggestion: This is an elegant company dessert. However, because of the sugar content it is unsuitable for a diabetic diet.

LEMON LOAF

½ cup	raisins	125 mL
⅓ cup	skim milk	75 mL
¼ cup	soft margarine	60 mL
½ cup	sugar	125 mL
2	large eggs	2
1¼ cups	all-purpose flour	300 mL
1 tsp.	baking powder	5 mL
½ tsp.	salt	2 mL
2 tbsp.	lemon juice	30 mL
2 tbsp.	honey	30 mL
2 tbsp.	lemon juice	30 mL

Spray a 5 x 9" (13 x 23 cm) loaf pan with nonstick spray. Soak raisins in the skim milk. Cream margarine and sugar until light and fluffy. Add the eggs and beat well, for 30 seconds. Sift the dry ingredients together. Drain the raisins and add the milk and dry ingredients, alternately, to the batter, beginning and ending with the dry ingredients. Fold in **first amount** of lemon juice and all of the raisins. Pour into prepared loaf pan. Bake at 350°F (180°C) for 50 minutes. Cool 10 minutes and remove from pan. Combine **second amount** of lemon juice with honey. Heat over hot water for a minute to thin the honey. Prick the loaf all over with a toothpick or skewer. Spoon the honey-lemon mixture all over the loaf and allow it to soak in.

LEMON LOAF (Cont'd.)

MICROWAVE INSTRUCTIONS:

Prepare batter as above. Pour into a microwave tube pan, that has been sprayed with a nonstick spray. Cover with waxed paper and microwave on **medium** 10-12 minutes, rotating every 3 minutes. A toothpick should come out clean when inserted into the center of the cake, if it is done. Let stand for 10 minutes then invert on a cake plate. Prick all over with a toothpick. Combine the **second amount** of lemon juice with honey in a small bowl. Microwave on **high** for 15 seconds to thin honey. Spoon over the hot cake and allow to soak in.

Yield: 12 slices

1 Slice

		Food Groups
Calories	155	
Protein	3 g	1 Bread
Total Fat	5 g	1 Fruit
Saturated Fat	1 g	1 Fat
Carbohydrate	27 g	
Cholestrol	43 mg	
Sodium	131 mg	

Variation: Poppy Seed Loaf. Substitute ½ cup (125 mL) poppy seeds for the raisins. Make as above.

CALIFORNIA FRUIT CAKE

2 cups	seeded raisins*	500 mL
	hot water	
1 cup	coarsley chopped dates	250 mL
2 cups	quartered dried apricots	500 mL
½ cup	diced dried figs (about 4)	125 mL
¼ cup	dried banana chips	60 mL
¼ cup	diced, dried pineapple	60 mL
1 cup	coarsley chopped pecans	250 mL
1 cup	slivered almonds	250 mL
¾ cup	flour	175 mL
⅓ cup	loosely packed brown sugar	75 mL
½ tsp.	baking powder	2 mL
3	large eggs	3
1 tsp.	vanilla extract	5 mL
½ tsp.	lemon extract	2 mL
2 tbsp.	molasses	30 mL

*Soak the raisins in hot water while cutting up other fruits and nuts. Drain well before adding to other fruits.

Spray 2, 5 x 9" (13 x 23 cm) loaf pans with nonstick spray. Line with waxed paper and spray the paper as well. In a large bowl, combine all fruits and nuts, including drained raisins. Combine flour, brown sugar and baking powder; stir to blend. Add to fruit and mix well, so fruits are separated and not in clumps. Beat eggs; add extracts and molasses. Stir well to blend. Add to fruit mixture and stir well to blend. Spoon batter into prepared pans, spreading evenly. Bake at 300°F (150°C) for 1 hour, 20 minutes, or until cake tester inserted in the middle comes out clean. Cool on wire rack for 10 minutes before inverting and removing pans. Peel off paper and allow to cool. Wrap in foil and refrigerate. Will keep for about 2 months.

CALIFORNIA FRUIT CAKE
(Cont'd.)

MICROWAVE INSTRUCTIONS:

Spray a large microwave tube pan with nonstick spray. Line the bottom with waxed paper and spray it. Prepare the batter exactly as instructed above. Microwave on **medium** for 15-18 minutes, or until a cake tester inserted in the middle of the cake comes out clean. Let rest for 10 minutes before inverting onto wire rack. Remove the pan and the waxed paper and cool. Wrap in foil and refrigerate. Will keep for 2 months.

Yield: 40 slices

1 Slice

		Food Groups
Calories	140	
Protein	2 g	2 Fruit
Fat	4 g	1 Fat
Saturated Fat	1 g	1 Calorie Poor
Carbohydrate	26 g	
Cholestrol	23 mg	
Sodium	10 mg	

Note: The fat content is in the nuts. This is lovely to have on hand over the holidays and is perfect for someone watching their cholesterol and/or sodium.

COCOA ROLL

1 cup	cake flour	250 mL
1 tsp.	baking powder	5 mL
¼ tsp.	salt	1 mL
¼ cup	dry cocoa	60 mL
¼ tsp.	cinnamon	1 mL
¼ tsp.	cream of tartar	1 mL
3	eggs	3
⅞ cup	granulated sugar	225 mL
1 tsp.	vanilla	5 mL
⅓ cup	water	75 mL

Grease a 15 x 10 x 1" (37 x 25 x 2 cm) jelly roll pan. Line with greased waxed paper. Sift first 6 ingredients together in a bowl. In a deep bowl, beat eggs until thick and lemon colored. Beat in sugar gradually. Blend in water and vanilla. Fold in the sifted dry ingredients slowly. Pour into prepared pan. Bake at 375°F (190°C) for 15 minutes, or until cake springs back when touched lightly. Generously dust a clean dish towel with sifted icing sugar. Turn cake out onto towel. Peel off waxed paper. With long edge away from you, roll towel and cake towards you, as tightly as possible. Place on a rack to cool. When cooled, unroll and spread with ¾ recipe for Fresh Fruit Topping, page 162 (save ¼ for a dollop on the top) and any of suggested fillings below. Nutritional analysis includes the Fresh Fruit Topping only.

Yield: 20 slices

1 Slice

Calories	98	FoodGroups
Protein	2 g	1 Bread
Total Fat	2 g	½ Fat
Saturated Fat	1 g	
Carbohydrate	17 g	
Cholesterol	36 mg	
Sodium	41 mg	

Serving Suggestion: After the cake has cooled, it can be cut into 5 sections, rolled up in waxed paper, placed in a plastic bag and frozen. Suggested fillings: sliced fresh fruit, strawberries, kiwi, banana, etc. or chopped nuts. A bit of rum in the Fresh Fruit Topping is great. Use your imagination!

COCOA SNACKIN' CAKES

1 cup	whole-wheat flour	250 mL
3 tbsp.	brown sugar, lightly packed	45 mL
2 tbsp.	dry cocoa	30 mL
½ tsp.	baking powder	2 mL
½ tsp.	baking soda	2 mL
2 tbsp.	chopped nuts	30 mL
1	small banana, mashed	1
⅓ cup	soured milk or buttermilk*	75 mL
2 tbsp.	salad oil	30 mL

*To sour milk, add 1 tsp. (5 mL) vinegar to the ⅓ cup (75 mL) milk and set aside while measuring other ingredients.

Spray 8 medium muffin cups with a nonstick spray or line with paper baking cups. Sift dry ingredients together in a medium-sized bowl. Stir in the nuts. Combine banana, milk and salad oil. Stir into dry ingredients just until moistened. Divide batter evenly among 8 muffin cups. Bake at 375°F (190°C) for 10 minutes. Serve warm.

MICROWAVE INSTRUCTIONS:

Line a microwave muffin pan with 4 paper baking cups (leave 2 spaces empty). Prepare batter as above. Divide evenly among baking cups. Microwave at medium for 3-4 minutes, rotating at ½ time. Test for doneness with a toothpick. Repeat baking procedure for 4 more cakes. Serve warm.

Yield: 8 servings

1 Serving

		Food Groups
Calories	124	1 Bread
Protein	3 g	1 Fat
Total Fat	5 g	
Saturated Fat	0 g	
Carbohydrate	19 g	
Cholesterol	0 mg	
Sodium	126 mg	

Serving Suggestion: A light tasty treat to serve with coffee or tea.

OATMEAL BUTTONS

These little gems are so nice when you want just a little something with a cup of tea or a glass of milk

2	eggs, separated	2
¾ cup	sugar	175 mL
1 tbsp.	melted margarine or butter	15 mL
1 tsp.	vanilla	5 mL
2⅛ cups	rolled oats	530 mL
2 tsp.	baking powder	10 mL
½ tsp.	salt	2 mL
½ tsp.	cinnamon	2 mL

Beat egg whites in a small bowl and set aside. Beat the egg yolks in a medium bowl. Stir in sugar, melted margarine and vanilla. Mix well. Combine all dry ingredients and add to egg yolk mixture. This will take some persistence. Fold in egg whites. Drop by teaspoonfuls onto a cookie sheet sprayed with nonstick spray. Bake at 400°F (200°C) for 10 minutes. Remove to a cooling rack immediately, to prevent crumbling.

Yield: 42 cookies

1 Cookie

Calories	43	**Food Groups**
Protein	1 g	½ **Bread**
Total Fat	1 g	
Saturated Fat	0	
Carbohydrate	8 g	
Cholesterol	14 mg	
Sodium	20 mg	

MERINGUE SHELLS

Many of us are intimidated by meringue shells. We shouldn't be. They are easy to make and, best of all, if you make them just slightly smaller than a coffee can, you can store them for 3 weeks or more. Handy to have to whip up a quick dessert.

2	egg whites at room temperature	2
½ cup	sugar	125 mL
⅛ tsp.	cream of tartar	0.5 mL
½ tsp.	vanilla extract	2 mL

In a deep bowl, beat the egg whites until frothy. Add the cream of tartar. Continue beating, adding the sugar 2 tbsp. (30 mL) at a time. Beat until stiff peaks form. Beat in vanilla. If you have a cookie sheet with a shiny buttom, use it, or cover a cookie sheet with foil, shiny side up. Spoon the meringue in mounds on the cookie sheet. Shape into 3" (7 cm) dishes, with the back of a spoon. Bake in a 275°F (100°C) oven for 30 minutes. Turn oven off, **do not open door,** and leave overnight. Meringues should be cooked and dry by morning. Store, with waxed paper between each, in a coffee can.

Yield: 8 shells

1 Shell

Calories	63	**Food Groups**
Protein	1 g	3 tsp. sugar
Total Fat	0 g	
Saturated Fat	0 g	
Carbohydrate	15 g	
Cholesterol	0 mg	
Sodium	20 mg	

Serving Suggestions: Fill with sweetened fresh fruit and top with Fresh Fruit Topping, page 162, or sweetened whipped cream, if you can afford the calories and saturated fat! These are unsuitable for a diabetic diet.

CHOCOLATE CHIP KISSES

We make these little gems every Christmas. They quite literally will melt in your mouth!

2	egg whites at room temperature	2
⅔ cup	sugar	150 mL
1 tsp.	vanilla extract	5 mL
⅛ tsp.	salt	0.5 mL
1 cup	chopped pecans	250 mL
6 oz. pkg.	tiny chocolate chips	170 g

Beat egg whites in a deep bowl until soft peaks form. Beat in sugar, 2 tbsp. (30 mL) at a time. Beat in vanilla and salt. Continue to beat until stiff peaks form. Fold in pecans and chocolate chips. On shiny side of cookie sheet or foil-covered cookie sheet, drop 'kisses' by the ½ tsp. (2 mL). You should have 2 cookie sheets full, or about 75 total. Preheat oven to 350°F (180°C). **Put both sheets in the oven, close door and turn off the heat. Leave undisturbed overnight.** If sticky in the morning, leave out in the air to dry for an hour before removing with a spatula.

Yield: 75

1 Cookie

Calories	31	**Food Groups**	
Protein	0 g	½ Fat	
Total Fat	2 g	1 tsp. sugar	
Saturated Fat	0 g		
Carbohydrate	4 g		
Cholesterol	0 mg		
Sodium	10 mg		

See photograph opposite.

Pears in Port Sauce, page 161
Chocolate Chip Kisses, page 160

PEARS IN PORT SAUCE

⅓ cup	port wine	75 mL
1 tbsp.	white sugar	15 mL
2 tsp.	lemon juice	10 mL
1 tsp.	grated orange rind	5 mL
2	bosc pears	2

In a saucepan, combine the wine, sugar, lemon juice and orange rind. Bring to a boil. Wash pears and cut in half, removing cores. Place cut side down in the sauce. Simmer just until pears are tender. Remove them to a serving dish. Continue to cook sauce until reduced by half. Spoon over the pears. Serve at room temperature.

MICROWAVE INSTRUCTIONS:

In a shall casserole with a lid, combine the wine, sugar, lemon juice and orange rind. Cover and microwave on **high** for 1 minute. Wash pears and cut in half, removing the cores. Place cut side down in the sauce. Microwave on **medium,** covered, for 5 minutes, turning at ½ time. Remove pears to serving dishes. Microwave sauce, uncovered, on **high** for 3 minutes, or until sauce is reduced by half. Spoon over the pears. Serve at room temperature.

Yield: 2 servings

1 Serving

		Food Groups
Calories	159	
Protein	1 g	2 Fruit
Total Fat	1 g	2 tsp. sugar
Saturated Fat	0 g	
Carbohydrate	32 g	
Cholesterol	0 mg	
Sodium	5 mg	

Serving Suggestion: This is a lovely light dessert when the meal has been a bit filling. If you feel it needs a topping, may we suggest the Fresh Fruit Topping, page 162.

See photograph page 160A.

FRESH FRUIT CUP TOPPING

4 oz.	light cream cheese	125 g
½ cup	2% MF yogurt	125 mL
¼ tsp.	vanilla	1 mL
½ tbsp.	fresh lime juice (optional)	7 mL
	artificial sweetener to equal	
	3 tbsp. (45 mL) sugar	

Whip cream cheese; add remaining ingredients. Mix with an electric mixer until light and fluffy. Store in refrigerator.

Yield: 16 servings of 1 tbsp. (15 mL) each

1 Serving

Calories	19	**Food Groups**	
Protein	0 g	1 Calorie Poor	
Fat	1 g		
Saturated Fat	0 g		
Carbohydrate	1 g		
Cholesterol	0 mg		
Sodium	3 mg		

Serving Suggestions: This topping adds variety to a mixed fresh fruit cup or sliced strawberries, baked apple, poached pear, calorie-reduced gelatin desserts, or a slice of Angel Food Cake (which is equal to 1 Bread).

Note: A double portion should be counted as half Fat Group, per serving.

BLUEBERRY GRUNT

1 cup	blueberries, fresh or frozen	250 mL
2 tsp.	sugar	10 mL
½ tsp.	lemon juice	2 mL
3 tbsp.	water	45 mL
⅛ tsp.	mace or allspice	0.5 mL
¼ cup	flour	60 mL
½ tsp.	sugar	2 mL
¾ tsp.	baking powder	4 mL
3 tbsp.	skim milk	45 mL

In a small saucepan, combine blueberries, sugar, lemon juice, water and mace or allspice. Bring to a boil and simmer for 3 minutes. In a small bowl, sift together the flour, sugar and baking powder. Add the skim milk and stir, just until blended, with a fork. Make 2 dollops of the batter on top of the blueberries. Cover and simmer until dumpling top is cooked through, about 15 minutes. Cool slightly to thicken before serving.

MICROWAVE INSTRUCTIONS:

In a small microwave casserole, combine blueberries, sugar, lemon juice, water and mace or allspice. Cover and microwave on **high** for 3 minutes, a little longer if using frozen berries. In a small bowl, sift together the flour, sugar and baking powder. Add the skim milk and stir, just until blended, with a fork. Make 2 dollops of the batter on top of the blueberries. Cover and microwave on **high** for 2 minutes. Cool slightly before serving.

Yield: 2 servings

1 Serving

		Food Groups
Calories	140	Food Groups
Protein	3 g	1 Fruit
Total Fat	0 g	1 Bread
Saturated Fat	0 g	
Carbohydrate	32 g	
Cholesterol	0 mg	
Sodium	26 mg	

Serving Suggestion: Warm Blueberry Grunt is a lovely breakfast, for a change. Just add a glass of milk!

ORANGE CUSTARD

1 tbsp.	diced orange peel	15 mL
1 tsp.	granulated sugar	5 mL
2 tbsp.	water	30 mL
1	egg	1
1 tbsp.	granulated sugar	15 mL
⅔ cup	skim milk	150 mL
3 tbsp.	skim milk powder	45 mL
¼ tsp.	vanilla	1 mL

Peel 4 very thin strips from an orange, be sure you have no white, only the peel. Dice finely and combine with the first amount of sugar and water in a small saucepan. Simmer for about 5 minutes, or just until the water evaporates and the peel is syrupy. Cool. Combine the egg and second amount of sugar in a bowl and beat slightly. Add milk, skim powder and vanilla. Beat just to combine. Divide the orange peel between 2 custard cups sprayed with nonstick spray. Divide the egg mixture between the 2 cups. Stir slightly to disperse the orange peel. Set the custard cups in a pan of warm water coming half way up the sides of the cups. Bake at 350°F (180°C) for 30-35 minutes. Test for doneness by inserting a knife blade carefully into the center of the custard. If the blade comes out clean, the custards are done. Chill.

MICROWAVE INSTRUCTIONS:

Peel 4 very thin strips from an orange, be sure you have no white only the peel. Dice finely and combine with the first amount of sugar and water in a microwave-safe bowl. Microwave on **high** for 3-4 minutes, or until the water has evaporated and peel is syrupy. Cool. Combine the egg and second amount of sugar in a bowl and beat slightly with a fork. Combine the milk and skim milk powder in a glass measure and microwave on **high** to just below a boil. Stir in the vanilla. Stir into the egg mixture slowly. Divide the peel between 2 custard cups. Divide the egg mixture between the 2 cups and stir to disperse orange peel. Microwave on **low** for 8-10 minutes. Test for doneness by inserting a knife blade carefully into the center of the custard. If the blade comes out clean, the custards are done. Chill.

Yield: 2 Servings

164

ORANGE CUSTARD (Cont'd.)

1 Serving

Calories	140	**Food Groups**
Protein	9 g	½ R Meat
Total Fat	3 g	1 Milk
Saturated Fat	1 g	1 tsp. sugar
Carbohydrate	18 g	
Cholesterol	110 mg	
Sodium	120 mg	

Serving Suggestion: A lovely way to meet one's calcium requirements. This would be an excellent dessert to serve with the Pasta Primavera, page 112. May be unmolded and surrounded with orange segments.

VARIATIONS:

CARAMEL CUSTARD: Omit orange peel, water and first amount of sugar. Put 1 tsp. (5 mL) brown sugar in the bottom of each custard cup before adding the milk and egg mixture. **Do not stir!** When you unmold, the caramel syrup will cover the custard.

MOCHA CUSTARD: Omit the orange peel, water and first amount of sugar. Stir 1 tsp. (5 mL) instant coffee into 1 tsp. (5 mL) hot water. Mix with the egg and milk mixture before pouring into the custard cups.

THREE AT ONCE: Triple the basic recipe of egg, sugar, milk, skim milk powder and vanilla. In 2 custard cups, place the orange peel, in 2 more the brown sugar. In the last 2, the dissolved instant coffee. Divide the egg mixture among the cups. Stir the orange and the mocha. **DO NOT STIR THE CARAMEL.** Increase baking time to 40-50 minutes.. Increase microwave time to 11-13 minutes, rearranging every 3 minutes and testing for doneness at the end of 11 minutes. Remove any that are done.

KEY LIME PIE

CRUST:

¾ cup	very fine gingersnap crumbs	175 mL
1 tbsp.	melted margarine	15 mL

FILLING:

2	limes	2
2 tsp.	grated lime rind	10 mL
10 oz.	can sweetened condensed milk	300 mL
2 drops	green food coloring (optional)	2 drops
1 tsp.	unflavored gelatin	5 mL
¼ cup	water	60 mL
⅔ cup	low-fat plain yogurt	150 mL

Crust: Combine the gingersnap crumbs with the margarine and mix well. Press onto the sides and bottom of a pie plate. Bake in a 350°F (160°C) oven for 6-8 minutes. Cool and fill as following instructions.

Filling: Grate the rind of the limes before cutting them in half and extracting the juice. Combine the juice and ½ the rind with condensed milk, beating until smooth and thickened. Stir in 2 drops of green food coloring, if you wish your pie to be green as on the cover. Sprinkle the gelatin on the water. Heat over boiling water or microwave on **high** 1 minute to dissolve gelatin, stirring to dissolve the gelatin. Cool slightly before stirring into the milk mixture. Gently stir in the yogurt and pour the filling into the prepared pie shell. Sprinkle the remaining grated rind over the filling and chill several hours before serving.

KEY LIME PIE (Cont'd.)

MICROWAVE INSTRUCTIONS:

Prepare crumb crust as above using a glass pie plate. Crust must be of uniform thickness to avoid burning in any one spot. Microwve at **medium** 4-5 minutes, rotating every minute. Cool and fill as above.

Yield: 8 servings

1 Serving

Calories	222	**Food Groups**
Protein	5 g	2 Bread
Total Fat	7 g	1 Fat
Saturated Fat	3 g	
Carbohydrate	36 g	
Cholesterol	16 mg	
Sodium	141 mg	

Serving Suggestion: This is what we call a "special occasion dessert." It is higher in calories than most of our desserts, but once in a while these things are O.K. You might try having a very light dinner (Wine Poached Trout, page 90 or Roast Turkey, page 109) to balance it all out.

See photograph on front cover.

NOTES

INDEX

169

INDEX

INDEX

INDEX

Additional Healthy Lifestyle Books by Lee Harvey & Helen Chambers

Lose Weight & Love It! — Family Favorites on a Diet
by Lee Harvey and Helen Chambers

Low-calorie, computer-analyzed recipes with conventional and microwave cooking instructions provide an easy guide to weight loss. The dietitian authors operate a successful nutrition and weight-loss clinic which allows Linguini with Clam Sauce, Macaroni and Cheese, Shepherd's Pie and Chocolate Mousse. Follow the 5-Step Guide to designing a weight loss plan to fit your lifestyle.

Retail $14.95 Can.
      $11.95 U.S.
188 pages   6" x 9"
8 colored photographs
printed cerlox binding
ISBN 0-9692369-1-3

Eat Light & Love It! — Cholesterol Control Guide/ Low-Calorie, Low-Fat Recipes
by Lee Harvey and Helen Chambers

Delicious new recipes, with an emphasis on controlling cholesterol, are included in this healthy eating guide. Up-to-date information about cholesterol and your diet is featured. The success of "Lose Weight & Love It!" and the demands from clients in the authors' nutrition clinic have resulted in this new selection of taste-tempting, low-calorie recipes. Conventional and microwave cooking, etc.

Retail $14.95 Can.
      $11.95 U.S.
188 pages   6" x 9"
8 colored photographs
printed cerlox binding
ISBN 0-9692369-2-1

NOTES

Share *"Light & Easy For Two!"* with a Friend

Order *LIGHT & EASY FOR TWO! EAT LIGHT & LOVE IT! or LOSE WEIGHT & LOVE IT!* at $14.95 per book plus $2.50 (total order) for mailing.

Light & Easy For Two! _____ × $14.95 = $ _____

Eat Light & Love It _____ × $14.95 = $ _____

Lose Weight & Love It _____ × $14.95 = $ _____

Add Mailing Charge _____ $ __2.50__

Sub Total: _____ $ _____

In Canada add 7% GST _____ .07 × Sub Total = $ _____

Total enclosed _____ $ _____

Name: _____

Street: _____ City: _____

Province/State: _____ Postal Code/Zip Code: _____

Make cheque payable to: **H.C. Publishing**
P.O. Box 3231 Station "D"
Ottawa, Ontario, Canada K1P 6H8

Price is subject to change.
Price in U.S. dollars $11.95 — postage $2.50

For fund raising or volume rates, contact **H. C. Publishing.**

Share *"Light & Easy For Two!"* with a Friend

Order *LIGHT & EASY FOR TWO! EAT LIGHT & LOVE IT! or LOSE WEIGHT & LOVE IT!* at $14.95 per book plus $2.50 (total order) for mailing.

Light & Easy For Two! _____ × $14.95 = $ _____

Eat Light & Love It _____ × $14.95 = $ _____

Lose Weight & Love It _____ × $14.95 = $ _____

Add Mailing Charge _____ $ __2.50__

Sub Total: _____ $ _____

In Canada add 7% GST _____ .07 × Sub Total = $ _____

Total enclosed _____ $ _____

Name: _____

Street: _____ City: _____

Province/State: _____ Postal Code/Zip Code: _____

Make cheque payable to: **H.C. Publishing**
P.O. Box 3231 Station "D"
Ottawa, Ontario, Canada K1P 6H8

Price is subject to change.
Price in U.S. dollars $11.95 — postage $2.50

For fund raising or volume rates, contact **H. C. Publishing.**